The Tipping-Point of History

EIR Contents

www.larouchepub.com   Volume 45, Number 17, April 27, 2018

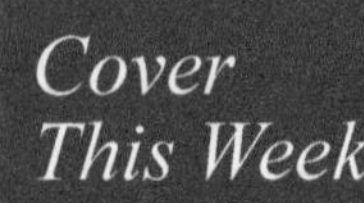

*Cover
This Week*

*Photo of Earth
from Apollo 17.*

NASA

THE TIPPING-POINT OF HISTORY

ZEPP-LAROUCHE WEBCAST

False Flags, Fake News, Regime Change in Washington Exposed as Made in London

This is the edited transcript of the April 19, 2018 Schiller Institute New Paradigm webcast, an interview with the founder of the Schiller Institutes, Helga Zepp-LaRouche. She was interviewed by Harley Schlanger. A video *of the webcast is available.*

Harley Schlanger: Hello. I'm Harley Schlanger from the Schiller Institute. Welcome to this week's international webcast, featuring our President and founder Helga Zepp-LaRouche.

When we spoke with you last, we were possibly on the verge of a world war breaking out. One of the things that Helga emphasized last week, was that if we could get through this time, there would be an opportunity to take down the British Imperial apparatus which is behind the war drive. In the last few days we've seen an exposure of the lies coming from Britain. We have been out front exposing those lies, but now various institutions of governments, even in some media, are catching on.

So I think this is where we should start: We're now at a point where these exposés give us the opportunity we have needed for a long time, to take apart the British Imperial geopolitical apparatus. Helga, what's the potential for that happening, now?

Helga Zepp-LaRouche: It is quite amazing. More and more countries, governments, and also political forces are speaking out against the fact that many of these operations were orchestrated by the British. The role of the British govern-

ment and MI6 in Russiagate is fully in the limelight; the whole Skripal affair is also now basically being questioned by many as to who really perpetrated the attack; and the narrative of chemical weapons use by the Assad government, which was the supposed reason for the recent military strikes against Syria, is also falling apart. So I think there is an increasing awareness that there is one country which is really on the war path against Russia, and—despite nice words, by implication, also against China. And that I think is a very important turn.

As a matter of fact, this afternoon, there was a press briefing by the Russian Foreign Ministry spokeswoman Maria Zakharova, who went into a lengthy description of all the British operations, starting with operations against the Soviet Union, the British work with the fascists in Ukraine, and then also more recent cases. So it's a long history, and I think one has to really look at the speech which British Prime Minister Theresa May made last November, where she talked about a new "Global Brit-

HM Government

Theresa May, UK Prime Minister (left), with her husband Philip May (right).

ain." May just appointed a new Chief of the Defense Staff, Gen. Sir Nicholas Carter, who is making a complete tirade against Russia, claiming Russia is involved in all evil deeds, from corruption to cyber-attacks. It's really a rampage. The force behind the war drive is the British government—self-exposed, acting now in its own name, but also the neo-cons, who are trying to manipulate President Trump into their cause, despite the fact that Trump was elected on the basis of his promise not to conduct interventionist wars any more.

So it's really a huge battle that's going on. But I think the exposure of all of these British lies is a new phenomenon, and it also makes those governments that gave unconditional support to the military strikes against Syria, look really bad. They lost all credibility, because they don't care for truth, and when they join in these groundless attacks against Russia, I think it will lead further to the collapse of the Western system, because many people see that these governments cannot be trusted. That's not a good thing, but that's what's happening.

Schlanger: Before we go into some of the specifics, it's important for you to identify for our viewers, the cause of this whole operation, because you've taken the lead in making sure people understand that this is not just mistakes being made, but an *intent*. If you look at the common purpose behind Russiagate, the Skripal affair, the Douma events, it is good to review here the essential argument being put forward by people like May, Nick Carter, the British empire, and the neo-cons in the United States.

Zepp-LaRouche: With the collapse of the Soviet Union, these forces thought that they could impose a unipolar world, get rid of all governments opposing such a system by regime change, color revolution, interventionist wars, which is what we have seen, especially in the 16 years of Bush Jr. and Obama. Obama

even said that Russia was just a regional power. Nobody expected Russia to fully return to the world stage, which Putin succeeded in doing, by turning around much of Russia's economy, but also by re-establishing a strategic balance with the West, with NATO.

China's rise was also underestimated by these same arrogant people, and now you have a flood of articles about the "new rise of China," or the "new proposals of the New Silk Road." These developments are not new; they have been going on almost five years.

You are seeing right now a realization, by the geopolitical faction of the neo-cons in the United States; the Democrats, who are mostly acting as neo-cons also; and the geopolitical British faction in Europe, that they are really in a rearguard battle, trying to prevail with their system, when their system is clearly inferior, outdated, and not attractive to many countries in the world, which see it much more advantageous to work with China and also Russia, in building up their own economies. This is really the battle, and it is very dangerous to the extent the lies being used by the British and being seconded by France's President Macron are accepted. They've gotten Trump temporarily roped into this scheme. I think the more these lies are exposed, the less they are effective, and the less is the danger of their being repeated in some new dirty trick.

European Opinion Opposes Syrian Bombing

Schlanger: One of the issues that the Russians in particular have been pursuing, is demanding a full investigation, both of the Skripal affair and the alleged April 7 chemical attack in Douma, Syria. There is a team from the Organization for the Prohibition of Chemical Warfare (OPCW) that's gone into Syria to take a look, and this is causing a real panic from the British, isn't it?

Zepp-LaRouche: Especially now that some of their own people, such as Robert Fisk from the *Inde-*

pendent, but also some former ambassadors, all point to the fact that the White Helmets outfit is really a terrorist organization; they work as humanitarian first responders by day, but turn into killers by night. This was the formulation used by one of the most famous Chinese journalists, Yang Rui. Also former British ambassador to Syria Peter Ford, and Craig Murray, former British ambassador to Uzbekistan, and also even some former military—are all asking the question, *cui bono*, who benefits? Assad surely had no motive to use chemical weapons in Douma. Why would Assad do that? His ally, Russia, stated that under Russian supervision Syria got rid of all its chemical weapons, and therefore why would Assad risk the relationship with Russia by using chemical weapons? Also, the timing of the alleged attack would not make any sense, either, because Assad was already almost in total control of the major parts of Syria, so why would he, at a point that he's winning, risk bringing down the thunder of Western anger against him?

No, the *cui bono* is clearly on the side of those who want to disrupt that process. The White Helmets are not only completely a terrorist organization working with al-Qaeda and some other groupings, but they are also financed by the British government, they are financed by the State Department's USAID, and there have even been reports that they were instigated to speed up this phony scenario in order to create a pretext for the missile attack.

So this is all coming out. While Theresa May is trying to play the super-hawk against Russia on the one hand, at the same time she is portraying herself as initiating a golden era between Great Britain and China. There was a telephone discussion in which President Xi talked about this idea of a "golden era" between the two countries, but then he said, that in the case of the alleged chemical weapons attack in Syria, there must be an absolutely thorough investigation to establish the truth of what really happened, which will stand up historically.

This was a very good move, and I think the possibility is good that the whole story will come out and be the subject of an international trial—because these are war crimes, what has happened. You cannot attack a sovereign country without UN Security Council agreement, or in self-defense. This missile attack was a clear violation of international law. It was a violation of the UN Charter. This is now causing a gigantic counter-reaction. I'm absolutely confident that the truth will come out.

Schlanger: Theresa May has a conflict of interest in terms of her relationship with the military-industrial complex. Why don't you fill our viewers in on this? I don't think it's gotten much coverage.

Zepp-LaRouche: She is married to Philip May, who is one of the top managers of an outfit called Capital Group, which happens to be the largest investor in BAE Systems, the largest weapons producer in Great Britain. Capital Group is also the second largest investor in Lockheed Martin. BAE, and probably also Lockheed Martin, made a great profit from these military attacks, because eight missiles produced by BAE Systems were used in the strike against Syria, and as a consequence, the stock prices of these companies skyrocketed.

So, if you have a prime minister who can declare war and her husband makes a profit from it, I think you have a clear case of conflict of interest, if not something worse. That should also be investigated. Yang Rui, the Chinese journalist I mentioned earlier, pointed to the fact that one should investigate the role of the military-industrial complex in this whole affair. That requires some limelight. Here you have a clear violation of international law, not only geopolitical reasons, but also personal profit-making, filling their own pockets.

Schlanger: As your husband Lyndon LaRouche once said, if you have something to hide, you shouldn't go out attacking other people, and certainly that's the case in dealing with May and the neo-cons. There was an attempt to get the European Union to support the U.S.-UK-France strike: That didn't go too well, did it?

Zepp-LaRouche: No. As a matter of fact, public opinion in Europe is, by a vast majority, against this, because people sense this is something horribly wrong and could lead to a war with Russia if it's not stopped. That's why the attempt by the EU foreign ministers, at their meeting on Monday to get an after-the fact resolution in support of these military strikes, did not function. Two important EU foreign ministers, from Italy and Belgium, opposed the resolution, arguing that it would unnecessarily aggravate the tensions with Russia. A number of European Union foreign ministers whose countries do not belong to NATO also opposed the resolution—Austria, Finland, Sweden, Cyprus, Malta, and Ireland.

The case of Austria is very important. Austria's Foreign Minister, Karin Kneissl, blasted this, insisting that it was a violation of international law and that Austria would absolutely not go along. As our viewers may know, a high-level delegation from the Austrian government has just returned from a very successful trip to China, where both the President and the Chancellor agreed with Xi Jinping that Austria and China would develop the closest relationship in Belt and Road cooperation.

Karin Kneissl, Austrian Foreign Minister.

So I think this is one more sign that the famous unity of the European Union does not exist. It doesn't exist on many issues, but fortunately also not on this one, and it just shows you that this EU construction is a terrible one, and the sooner it changes into something better, based on a higher principle, the better off the world will be.

Syria Looks to China

Schlanger: The White Helmet charge of Assad's use of chemical weapons came right after President Trump said twice in a week that he's preparing to move troops out of Syria. He wants the United States out, fulfilling his campaign promise. This was something that was picked up by Tucker Carlson at Fox News, Roger Stone in his commentary, and Pat Lang in his *Sic Semper-Tyrannis* blog article. After the attack, the U.S. Ambassador to the UN Nikki Haley, who is one of the hardest-core neo-cons (she was a supporter of Jeb Bush during the Presidential campaign, who somehow became the U.S. ambassador to the UN), appeared on the Sunday talk shows, saying the United States is going to stay in Syria. This was what French President Macron had boasted: that he had persuaded Trump to stay in Syria.

But the very next day Trump said that's not the case. He said that the United States is *not* going to stay in Syria, that he *does* want the troops out. Haley also said there will be new sanctions against Russia, but Trump walked back from that also, saying that's not the case. All this indicates a fairly intensive fight in the United States with the neo-cons doing everything they can to break any possibility of Trump and Putin talking.

You made the point, and I believe this was picked up in the Russia media, that Trump and Putin should meet as quickly as possible. How do you see something like that working?

Zepp-LaRouche: Well, it is very clear that Trump is in a very difficult position, because after the FBI raid on the offices of his personal lawyer, Michael Cohen, some are now worried that if Special Counsel Robert Mueller threatens Cohen with a life sentence in prison, as Alan Dershowitz, the constitutional lawyer, said, this would be aimed at turning Cohen into a canary who sings. When threatened with a life sentence in prison some people are not strong enough to stick to their loyalties, so this is a big concern. We have experienced these tactics sufficiently ourselves to know how this works.

Trump is surrounded by people who are trying to get him back to the Obama agenda. Roger Stone highlighted this problem in his recent article. He said that a concerted effort is being made by the neo-cons to lure Trump into scenarios that would force him to undo his election campaign promise to have a better relationship with Russia, and that would also damage his very good relationship with Xi Jinping.

So how do you outflank this? Everything—world

President Trump (left), French President Macron (right).

DIPLOMACY & DEFENCE

peace, the question of the future of mankind—depends on the most important countries, the United States, China, and Russia, having better relationships with each other. The best way to outflank all these petty and nasty attacks would be for the proposed meeting between Trump and Putin to be convened very soon. I'm absolutely convinced that these are two people, despite all the criticism one might have of either of them—I'm not saying that you have to support every step that either is taking—but it should be clear that both of them have proven many times over that they have better instincts. Without Putin's intervention in Syria, we would still have a total madhouse, and possibly a situation in Libya where terrorists would be completely in command. Putin has proven he can strategically outflank a seemingly hopeless situation.

Trump, despite all of this Russiagate, and unbelievable treason from many Republicans—the Democrats are pretty obvious—has proven himself to be quite resilient. I'm absolutely convinced that if these two were to get together in a lengthy summit meeting, they would come up with solutions for all of these problems, including the very important factor of the strategic partnership between China and Russia.

Sometimes, when you have a seeming contradiction, on a lower level, that seems impossible to solve, you just have to catapult the debate to a higher level. I think that if Putin and Trump were to meet very soon, this would be the most beneficial thing that could happen.

Schlanger: Where do things go from here in Syria? There was a statement issued the other day indicating that the Syrian government is looking at the Chinese

model and would like to have something like that. The Chinese have previously stated they're willing to come in and help reconstruct. Do you think it's possible that some of the European countries would get involved with China in the reconstruction effort in Syria?

Zepp-LaRouche: Italy is already doing it. We have discussed the Chinese-Italian cooperation in the Transaqua project. Some other nations are having a harder time. German Chancellor Mrs. Merkel, who has just fully endorsed the military strike, which was really a terrible thing, now says she wants to meet with President Putin to mediate between the United States and Russia, and also wants to play a role in the reconstruction of Syria. The position is still that Assad has to be gotten rid of. I don't see any indications that either the European Union or the German government is willing to change the failed paradigm of geopolitics.

The Syrian Ambassador to Beijing, on the other hand, said that Syria welcomes not only the role of China in the reconstruction of Syria, but that Syria wants to adopt the Chinese economic model because of the strong role of the state, and the fact that the state in the Chinese model protects the lower and poorer layers of society, the weaker layers of society. I think this is very good.

I wish that reasoning would enter the minds of some of the European governments and that they would join hands. I have not yet seen any sign of that yet. The German EU Commissioner for Budget and Human Resources, Günter Öttinger, has just said that Europe should not be a "fortress Europe," but Europe should bring development to Africa. But then he said that this should be done in order to not abandon the African continent to the Chinese, who only follow their egotistical aims. As long as that kind of idiotic thinking prevails, I don't think there is any solution.

Everyone should recognize what China is actually doing, and drop their prejudices. Compared to what the West is doing, the moral quality of what China is doing for its own people and for other nations is vastly superior.

Protect Cognitive Power of the People

Schlanger: I think it's fair to say the thinking of German industry and the *Mittelstand* is very far ahead of the German government, because they have welcomed Chinese involvement in Duisburg, Hamburg, and other places in Germany, where the Chinese are involved in a series of economic projects.

That brings us to China-U.S. relations. There was a very significant conference at the Brookings Institution just yesterday, in which we made a very important intervention. The topic was U.S.-China collaboration. What happened there, Helga? What can you tell us?

Zepp-LaRouche: The China Development Bank President was there and the China Report 2018 of the International Financial Forum (IFF) was presented at this Brookings event. One of our colleagues, Mr. Paul Gallagher, intervened and asked if it was not a good idea for the Chinese to help with infrastructure development in the United States, by using the Chinese holdings in U.S. Treasury bonds for investment in an infrastructure bank or a National Bank. The representative of the Brookings Institution was relatively surprised by such an approach. The Chinese panelist said it was a very important question and elaborated the idea. He fully endorsed the proposal, saying it would work very well.

It's very important that this was put on the table. This approach is what we have been proposing since 2015. The best possible way to put the U.S.-China relationship on a solid ground in terms of cooperation with the Belt and Road Initiative, would be Chinese investment in infrastructure in the United States, and in turn, have U.S. investments in joint ventures in the countries along the Belt and Road.

This discussion is absolutely urgent. You could get rid of the trade imbalance by having more trade, not just bilateral trade, but multilateral arrangements in the New Silk Road. This is very important.

Let us go back to the higher moral approach of China for a moment. I know some of our viewers will get upset about what I'm about to say, but I find it very, very useful that China has now launched several campaigns—one against Internet addiction; another against hip-hop, saying that hip-hop counterculture is just about white powder, women, sex, and violence. It promotes vulgar and low taste. Therefore it should not be on the Internet or TV channels, and should not be promoted. The Chinese government is calling on companies to promote healthy, beneficial, and truthful knowledge instead.

That's a good idea. The media is not the devil, it can be used to promote useful education instead of dragging people down with terrible violence and crime, and with awful ugliness, as is happening now in the West, in almost all movies and entertainment.

And China also has a campaign against quiz shows, because so many people are participating in banal quiz shows, saying this is also bad because it promotes Mammonism, which is money-greed, the search for riches. This is also being discouraged.

I think it's very good. Government should have a role in promoting the common good of the people. I think that the famous liberal model of the West has been hailed by some as the basis for legitimizing interventionist wars against countries that have different social models. I think it's much better if a government protects its own people against things which are clearly bad for the cognitive powers of its own population. Nothing would be lost if some of these terrible things did not exist. The youth would be in better shape. President Trump has taken up the issue of violent video games as one of the contributing factors in violence in the schools.

So I think this is one of the areas in which a useful cultural dialogue among countries could also take place: How do you protect your own population against such bad influences? This is a very important component of the strategic picture.

Courage of the World-Historical Individual

Schlanger: It would also be helpful if the media would stop lying. Helga, I have one more question for you, which is something that I get quite a bit in the radio interviews I'm doing: The events of the last couple of weeks have caused a lot of people who were hoping that we were moving into the New Paradigm, to lose their hope, lose their optimism. I had a number of people say to me, "How can you still be optimistic, when we're seeing the United States once again, whether willingly or not, getting suckered into a war and launching missiles against a sovereign state, which has not invited us in?"

I have my way of answering, but I'd like to hear your answer, because the sustaining of optimism in order to continue to fight for the good, is something people have to work on continuously. Otherwise, they're dragged down by the media.

How do you approach this situation, and why are you still optimistic?

Zepp-LaRouche: There is right now, in some European political layers, a big debate going on: Has the "deep state" in the United States won already, or are there still some options for Trump to stick to his announced policies?

Russian President Putin and President Trump meeting at G-20 Hamburg Summit, July 7, 2017.

Well, what people call the "deep state," which is what President Eisenhower had named the "military-industrial complex," combined with the intelligence services belonging to the British Empire faction, is still very strong.

But on the other hand, I think they have never been so exposed, and at a time when ordinary people have the feeling that everything is falling apart. Trust in government is collapsing, pensions are not seen as secure, there is fear of a new financial crisis much worse than 2008. In the West, people sense that there is no trustworthy institution they can turn to. In such a moment, when people realize who are the war-mongers, and that they're pushing war against Russia using lies, I think this can completely backfire. Once the lies are dismantled and the people pushing the lies are ostracized, I think there can be a return to decent international relations among nations, including reviving the UN Charter, and reviving international law. Sometimes you need a shock like the present experience, to move to a New Paradigm of international relations. I think that is absolutely something on the horizon.

I'm not sure it will go as peacefully as it did with the collapse of the Soviet Union, which, after all, without using tanks, agreed to the re-unification of Germany and the dissolution of the Warsaw Pact.

I don't have a clear idea of how the present collapse phase of the Western system will end up. There is a new dynamic; more and more countries are not going along any more. The East European countries, the Central European countries, the Balkan countries, the South European countries, Switzerland, Austria—all want to have a new kind of international relations. The more countries that have that kind of determination, and the more that in countries that are not yet there, such as Germany, France, and Great Britain, people mobilize and speak out to stick to the truth, change will occur. Many people are in motion right now. There are many appeals being circulated declaring, "we have to return to reason." We have to have good relationships with Russia and China. Without these two countries, no problem on this planet can be solved.

The more people engage in such discourse and get active, the better. That's why every time I speak to you, I call on you to join the Schiller Institute, help us get these video webcasts around, spread the word, and get active. I am absolutely convinced—in that sense I am a Leibnizian—believing that a great evil always generates the potential for an even greater good, because that's the law of the universe. I think the universe is made in such a way that there *is* a tremendous ability to improve, to become better, to have higher forms of existence. But it does require individual action. It's not a dialectical materialism, nor historical materialism, which proceeds all by itself, but there *is* such a thing as the combination of objective conditions and subjective intervention. The objective conditions do exist. They exist in the form of a New Paradigm promoted by all the countries participating in the Belt and Road Initiative. And if you add to that the subjective factor, which is the courage of the world-historical individual acting on the basis of his or her knowledge, I think there is great reason for hope that we can move humanity into a more safe historical period.

So therefore, I can only appeal to you: Join us! That's the best thing you can do.

Schlanger: Well, one institution which has earned your trust is the Schiller Institute. Since its founding in 1984, we've been ahead of the curve on virtually every single fight. And I think it's important, as Helga just said, to encourage you not to give up hope, but to find in yourself the strength to get out and wage this battle with us—to talk to people, to bring to them the light of reason, the New Silk Road Spirit.

Helga, thank you very much for joining us, and we'll be back again next week.

Zepp-LaRouche: Yes, till next week.

Political Crimes Committed by the UK

Briefing by Russian Foreign Ministry Spokesperson Maria Zakharova, Moscow, April 19, 2018

The following is the official translation of the transcript, *edited for language, with subheads added by EIR, of a one-hour portion of a briefing to the international press corps by Maria Zakharova, Director of the Information and Press Department of the Ministry of Foreign Affairs of the*

Maria Zakharova

Russian Federation. She is the official representative of the Ministry of Foreign Affairs.

Now I ask everyone to fasten their seatbelts. During a briefing on the OPCW [Organization for the Prohibition of Chemical Weapons] report held for the international diplomatic community on April 13, UK Ambassador to Russia Laurie Bristow said that "the Russian state has a record of state-sponsored assassinations including in the UK." It is not the first Russophobic statement made by a UK official, or, for that matter, not the first UK statement that is an offense to law, standards of decency or any morals. But it's not the main point.

Let's put aside morals and the law and talk about something different. Maybe the UK Ambassador does not know his own country's history, role, and involvement in processes that took place in other countries over the past

British rule in colonial India.

centuries. I don't think Mr. Bristow is to blame for the absence of law in the UK. He probably just doesn't know his country's history.

British Indian novelist Salman Rushdie wrote that "the trouble with the new Englishness is that their history happened overseas, so they don't know what it means." And so the island status that motivated Britain's imperial story in the first place has helped them distance themselves from all aspects of that story. I think now is the time to fill this cognitive vacuum and tell the world something about Britain's history and its international activities and their consequences.

Let us talk about state contracts, assassinations and Britain's reputation.

Modern History

Let's start with modern history. It is not a common subject, but Britain was one of the most ruthless metropolises in terms of the repressive actions it took in its colonies and dependent territories. On November 22, 2017, British journalist and writer Afua Hirsch wrote in *The Guardian* that "from the Norman conquest of Ireland in the 12th century, the English began imagining themselves as the new Romans, persuading themselves they were as duty-bound to civilize 'backward' tribes as they were destined to exploit their resources, land and labour." The British see "Britain's empire as a great moral achievement and its collapse as an act of casual generosity."

This accepted view of Britain's history completely overshadows some inconvenient facts. If the motive is what matters most of all, nobody wants to know the details. But today we will be speaking about details.

The establishment of concentration camps in the Boer War that later inspired the Nazis' death camps, the cultural annihilation of kingdoms and palaces from Ashanti to Beijing, British army massacres in Ireland and the devastation of Bengal, the industrial-scale exploitation of natural resources and the slave trade. These are only the most glaring facts.

The British in India

The impact of colonial rule in India was extremely devastating. In 1930, American historian Will Durant published a book about the history and life in India, *The Case for India*. His study of India brought him to the following conclusion: "The more I read the more I was filled with astonishment and indignation at the apparently conscious and deliberate bleeding of India by England throughout a hundred and fifty years. I began to feel that I had come upon the greatest crime in all history."

Britain has left fault lines across the globe, which is most acutely felt in the South Asian subcontinent, where a single nation was forcibly split into two in 1947. Today each of these parts is overcoming the consequences of the British colonial "legacy" on its own. Member of Parliament, former UN Under-Secretary General, Dr. Shashi Tharoor, an astute statesman who once ran for UN Secretary-General and deservedly enjoys respect the world over, has repeatedly stated that the British authorities suffer from "historical amnesia" as regards their imperial atrocities. One has to agree.

Speaking at Oxford on July 22, 2015, Dr. Shashi

Chatham House

Dr. Shashi Tharoor

Tharoor said: "India's share of the world economy when Britain arrived on its shores was 23%. By the time the British left, it was down to below 4%. Why? Simply because India had been governed for the benefit of Britain. Britain's rise for 200 years was financed by its depredations in India."

According to Dr. Tharoor, in fact, Britain's industrial revolution was actually premised upon the de-industrialization of India. Britain repeatedly provoked famine in India, which killed between 15 million and 29 million people. The best known famine was that in Bengal in 1943, when four million Indians died. You might think this is just journalistic speculation. But, no. Addressing the Speaker's Research Initiative on July 24, 2015, Indian Prime Minister Narendra Modi stressed that the discourse by Dr. Shashi Tharoor met the aspirations of his country's citizens. I am saying this to you, Mr. Bristow.

In his book *Inglorious Empire* released in 2017, Dr. Tharoor cited the atrocities of the British Empire, stating that the former British Prime Minister, Winston Churchill, should be regarded as one of the cruelest dictators of the 20th century. This is what Churchill said in a conversation with Secretary of State for India and Burma, Leopold Amery: "I hate Indians. They are a beastly people with a beastly religion. The famine was their own fault for breeding like rabbits." This is not merely what we are saying, nor are these our inventions. It's a fact.

Library of Congress

Sir Winston Churchill

Bengali Famine, 1943.

"The Devil's Wind" painting, British murder by cannon.

The Russian artist Vasily Vereshchagin has a famous painting, "The Devil's Wind." This is not a symbolic comparison. The canvas shows a type of execution invented by the British to crush the 19th century Sepoy Mutiny in India. The victim would be tied to a gun with his back to the muzzle and blown to pieces by a gunshot. This was one of the most barbaric punishments in the history of civilizations, aimed not so much at physical extermination or intimidation.

Even without it, the British had so many infernal instruments of torture and execution that this option doesn't seem so original and, honestly, was rather costly for the Brits. But from the religious and caste point of view this method of putting to death was absolutely unacceptable for Indians. Their bodies were blown to pieces and the dead were buried together regardless of caste, which is radically at variance with the Indian tradition.

Yet another episode of the same kind occurred in Amritsar, Punjab, on April 13, 1919, when 50 British troops under Brigadier-General Reginald Dyer fired their rifles without warning at pilgrims celebrating Baishakhi, the Punjabi harvest and New Year festival, at the centrally located Jallianwala Bagh public garden. The gathering was mostly made up of women and children. I would like to draw your attention to the fact that these British subjects were acting on direct orders of the British authorities. According to the British government, 379 people were killed and over 1,000 wounded. The Indian National Congress said 1,000 people were killed and 1,500 wounded. Regrettably, millions of Indians were to fall victim to the acts committed by the British authorities, including mass executions by firing squad, during at least several decades after these sad events.

British Concentration Camps in Africa

Africa has also suffered its share of British abuses. Some 13 million Africans were removed from the continent as slaves.

This has everything to do with Britain's reputation and the UK Ambassador's allegations regarding Russia.

Camp for prisoners to be shipped out during the Second Anglo-Boer War.

The number of Africans who died in that period is three or four times larger than the number of those who were removed from the continent. In other words, the overall number of victims runs into tens of millions of people. It is notable that English philosopher John Locke [1632-1704], who advanced the theory of civil society and whose works influenced those who wrote the U.S. Constitution, was a major investor in Britain's slave trade. It is a fact.

The British were among the first to invent concentration camps for civilians in the Boer War of 1899-1902. These camps were created for the civilians who were suspected of sympathizing with the rebels or who could help them. The British torched their farms and fields and slaughtered their cattle. Women and children were separated from men. All this happened long before WWII. The men were taken to outlying regions or Britain's other colonies, such as India or Ceylon.

When the world learned about this horrible invention of British military commander, Lord Kitchener, the British government published an official statement saying that the camps had been created to keep the peaceful population of the Boer Republics safe from harm's way, and the camps were renamed "refugee camps." This is remindful of the story of the White Helmets: take militants, extremists and terrorists, put white helmets on them with "Peace" written on these helmets, and then use them to stage provocations and present mobile phone footage of their crimes as evidence of the plight of the civilians who must be saved. Centuries have passed, yet nothing has changed. Prisoners are now called "guests of the Crown." Overall, 200,000 people, half of the white Boer population, was herded into the British camps, where about 30,000 of them died from disease and hunger.

There were British camps in Cyprus and in Palestine from the late 1930s to 1948, where Jewish refugees were sent and many executed.

British Field Marshal Horatio Herbert Kitchener.

The Notorious Special Air Service

Another dark page from Britain's history concerns the notorious Special Air Service (SAS) of the British Army, which have been used in over 30 local conflicts, mostly former British colonies, including Kenya and several other countries of southern Africa..

In particular, about 50 former SAS servicemen were included in the Rhodesian regiment that was to play a key role in the coup staged during the transfer of power to the indigenous population of Rhodesia (renamed Zimbabwe).

Historians believe that Britain is the world's leader when it comes to genocide, given the millions of innocent civilians that have been killed in British colonies.

According to different estimates, between 90-95% of aborigines were exterminated during the colonization of Australia. Indigenous Australians were not only killed but also used for experiments. The British deliberately infected them with various diseases, primarily pox.

The armed conflict between the British colonizers and the indigenous people of Tasmania, known as the Black War, all but exterminated Tasmanians in the early 19th century. Some British historians consider the war to have been a genocide. The British colonizers had official license to kill Tasmanians, with a bounty put on every person killed.

That has much to say to the question of international reputation.

Tasmanians were poisoned, driven out into the desert, where they died from hunger and thirst; they were hunted like wild animals. By 1835 only about 200 survived. They were simply moved to neighboring islands.

On the orders of the British authorities, genocide of Zulus was perpetrated in the Cape Colony in the 1870s, and in 1954-1961 of the Kikuyu people in Kenya. The British authorities massacred 300,000 Kikuyus and sent 1.5 million to work camps in retaliation for the kill-

'Nemesis' destroying Chinese junks in Anson's Bay, 1841.

ing of 32 white settlers by the local rebels. An account of these events is given in a book by Caroline Elkins titled *The Untold Story of Britain's Gulag in Kenya.* The Western media are reluctant and embarrassed to talk about it, but the personal story of the former U.S. President Barack Obama speaks volumes. We have read that his father was tortured by the British during the Kenya rebellion. Or is that story untrue?

Remember that the notorious Opium Wars were part of a longer process. London had been poisoned the Chinese people with drugs for decades. Britain organized a supply of opium to China, making fabulous profits. The operation also pursued the military-strategic aim of demoralizing the Chinese army and people to depriving them of the will to resist. In a bid to save his country, the Chinese Emperor in 1839 launched a massive operation to confiscate and destroy opium stocks in Canton. London retaliated by unleashing the Opium Wars. China was defeated and had to sign a crippling peace with Britain.

"As long as China remains a nation of *opium*-smokers there is not the least reason to fear that she will become a military power of any importance, as the habit saps the energies and vitality of the nation." This was how Richard Hurst, the British Consul in China, ended his speech to the Royal Opium Commission in 1895. It was not until 1905 that the Chinese authorities managed to adopt and start implementing a program to gradually ban opium.

Recent History: When London Was Vocal

And now for instances from recent history, when London was already vocal in upholding human rights, calling itself a bastion of democracy and freedom:

We have already described the suffering inflicted on India. This is not our question, this is common sense. Think of the suffering inflicted by the British authorities in the Middle East. One need hardly go to any length to argue that Britain, seeking to retain as much influence as possible in the region as it saw the colonial system crumble, made some moves which created a deep rift between the Arabs and the Jews. One need not go into historical details; it is enough to open the world map and look at the borders in the region as they were redrawn by the British after the collapse of the Ottoman Empire.

Borders were redrawn with no more care than drawing a line with a ruler. But this concerned the lives of whole nations. As a result, tribes, ethnic and religious communities and peoples were divided. The world is still reaping the fruit of that policy in the Middle East today. Yet, Britain is still very active on this issue.

One more interesting fact: According to the British national archives declassified in 2014, the British authorities made wide use of chemical weapons to put down the Arab rebellion in Mesopotamia (present-day Iraq) in the spring of 1920. Winston Churchill as

British troops entering Baghdad, 1916.

Britain's Secretary of State for War supported "the use of gas against uncivilized tribes." According to archives, Churchill ordered the use of thousands of mustard gas shells against the rebels. The anti-British rebellion in Iraq claimed between 6,000 and 10,000 lives, according to various sources, a negligible number from London's point of view, compared to other regions.

The Greeks, too, got their share of British brutality. In the spring of 1944, Britain crushed a revolt in the Greek army in Egypt. Many historians believe that the suppression of that revolt paved the way for, and was a prelude to the British invasion of Greece in December 1944 and the Civil War of 1946-1949. Of the 30,000 Greek officers and men in the Middle East, between 20,000 and 22,000 were imprisoned in British camps in Eritrea, Egypt, Sudan and Libya.

Continuing to the 1970s and Beyond

In the late 1960s and 1970s the British authorities evicted 1,500 indigenous people from the Chagos Archipelago in the Indian Ocean. At the United Nations, the British diplomats passed off the indigenous Ilua people as "contract workers." The reason was the U.S. desire to set up a military base on one of the islands. It was that simple.

Moreover, the whole archipelago was declared to be a marine reserve. In 2009, Wikileaks reported that the British government had backed the project to make sure that the continued attempts of deported islanders to return to their home island would fail. Ironically, the American military base on Diego Garcia Island was called Camp Justice. Sounds great.

Here is another example from recent history. The secret service of the British Armed Forces intentionally falsified reports on military crimes committed between 2010 and 2013 so as to conceal information on killings of civilians in Afghanistan. Unarmed Afghan civilians, who were regarded as potential Taliban militants, were killed, not detained as per the reports, during raids on their homes.

Launched in 2014, the investigation into war crimes in Afghanistan committed in 2010-2013 was code-named Operation Northmoor, with investigators establishing that the secret service in question had forged documents to shift the blame for killing unarmed civilians to the Afghan army.

This is apropos the question of international reputation, Mr. British Ambassador.

The investigators got hold of drone footage, the so-

SAS soldiers 'suspected' of executing unarmed Afghans and covering up potential war crimes

Special forces soldiers allegedly murdered civilians and planted guns on their bodies

called Kill TV, which clearly shows that it was the British, rather than their Afghan colleagues, who were firing at unarmed Afghans. According to *The Times* (July 2, 2017), the UK Defense Ministry intended to conceal these war crimes from the media, because it believed that the publication of the investigation's details could cause damage to national security, public confidence and collaboration with allies. At the same time, the UK top army brass described the evidence of mass killings that had been discovered during the investigation as reliable, very serious, and disastrous for the government. But no disaster ensued. The British authorities always have something to distract the attention of esteemed journalists.

On November 19, 2017, *The Sunday Times* published another story on SAS killings, specifically an admission by Major Chris Green, who had testified to an SAS unit killing three peaceful Afghans in cold blood, in the courtyard of their house in the village of Rahim, Nahr-e-Saraj, Helmand Province. The civilians had no connections with the Taliban.

Iraq 2003-2011

Now to Iraq. According to information from open sources, 326 criminal proceedings were instituted in connection with British military abuses during the Iraq war in 2003-2011, with charges brought against 1,500 persons. The compensations paid to the injured parties added up to £20 million.

It could be said that these are just isolated occurrences unrelated to official state strategy. After all, there is always an investigation following any wrongdoing. Well, there are investigations, of course, and people get punished. But the British government, which sanctions all these things, never suffers any punishment and, what is most important, is that all of this keeps happening again and again, year after year, decade after decade, century after century.

The media focused on an episode that happened in Basra in 2003. The British military detained two Iraqis for the alleged killing of two British snipers. They were kept in prison without charge or trial for several years. They were charged with murder only in 2006. But Iraq's Supreme Tribunal dropped the charges as unsubstantiated.

To minimize the number of lawsuits against the British military for crimes committed during military campaigns, the Tory annual conference in Birmingham held in October 2016 was presented with a government plan to grant British servicemen involved in conflicts abroad immunity from prosecution by the European Convention on Human Rights.

Espionage, Sabotage and Killing

Now let's move on to espionage operations and pinpoint sabotage and subversive acts. From time immemorial, representatives of Great Britain have been avid fans of various kinds of covert operations and targeted subversive acts against specific individuals as a way to secure political benefits for Great Britain. This predisposition is richly represented in their art, things like the James Bond 50th Anniversary Gold Collection. This may sound ridiculous unless you know that the author of the book series, Ian Fleming, had searched through the archives, so Agent 007 in fact has real prototypes. This anthology of crime, artfully described by writer and part-time naval intelligence officer Fleming is a light version for those who are not interested in historiography, who see archive work as boring or believe that materials there may have various interpretations and require additional checks.

Indeed, the Bondiana [the James Bond mythology] is a very symptomatic example of the British government's love of such things. Fleming died in 1964, but what he described lives and thrives. New James Bond episodes are regularly released, as everyone is used to the superhero. Times change, the actors and sets change,

Agent 007 in fact has real prototypes.

but the idea remains unchanged—a British agent, in the service of the Kingdom, gets nothing less than a "license to kill." Once again I repeat, this is not a fictional invention, but a result of work with archival materials. What we see in the Bondiana is actually taking place under the cover of MI5 and MI6.

Thanks to the films, people have a basic understanding of the license to kill concept—a term denoting the permission granted by the official government or a state agency to a secret agent who serves this authority to independently make a decision on the necessity and expediency of murder to achieve a certain goal. Once the mission is completed, the agent always returns to the base. We have seen that as well.

It is a pity that in normal life, to which we will now return, things are not so beautiful and dignified. Fleming did something brilliant: he took facts and packaged them beautifully. What we see is a very beautiful picture.

British Acts in Russia

And now getting back to reality. The following historical episodes are not fiction, they are facts. Some of them are proven, whereas others are highly likely hypotheses put forward by historians. But the key is that while as far back as a month and a half ago we did not use materials which are just hypotheses in official statements, with a helping hand from UK Prime Minister Theresa May who introduced the "highly likely" phrase to level an accusation of a most grave crime, why should we deny it to ourselves?

Scotland Yard historians have also maintained the complicity of British authorities in the murder of Grigory Rasputin. Michael Smith, a historian of the British intelligence, writes in his book, *SIX: A History of Britain's Secret Intelligence Service*, that in 1916, at the height of World War I, the British intelligence resident agent in Petrograd heard rumors that Grigory Rasputin was trying to conclude a separate peace treaty with Germany through the Tsarina. This fact worried the British a great deal. Captain Oswald Raymer of MI6 was dispatched to Petrograd to get information about the talks from Rasputin and eliminate him, if necessary. According to Michael Smith, the third bullet in Rasputin's head (the "official" murderers' testimony does not say anything about that) came from a .455 Webley, a British revolver, whereas the plotters' memoirs indicate that Prince Felix Yusupov fired a pocket-size Browning and Purishkevich—a Savage pistol. The following is a striking admission from the declassified correspondence of British intelligence agents. A friend of Captain Oswald Rayner wrote a letter to the British intelligence officer, John Scale, on December 24, 1916 saying: "Although matters have not proceeded entirely to plan, our objective has been achieved ... Rayner is attending to loose ends and will certainly contact you." A number of historians are convinced that the message refers to Rasputin's murder. In 2004, the BBC aired its documentary, "Who Killed Rasputin?" According to British journalists, the "glory" and the plot of the murder belong to Great Britain, whereas the Russian conspirators were merely actors or instruments.

There are similar versions regarding the murder of Russian Emperor Paul I, but I think this is a question to be addressed to historians.

Historians also write about the so-called Lockhart Conspiracy organized in 1918 by the heads of the diplomatic missions of Britain, France and the USA to Soviet Russia in order to overthrow the Bolsheviks. The conspiracy involved the chief of the British special mission, Robert Lockhart, French Ambassador Joseph Noulens, and U.S. Ambassador David Francis.

Grigory Rasputin

Patrice Lumumba

International Criminal Court

Mohammed Mossadegh (with cane), who successfully nationalized Anglo-Iranian Oil and was then overthrown by the British.

Robert Lockhart tried to bribe the Latvian Riflemen who were guarding the Kremlin. You know the rest of the story. The Latvians were supposed to be sent to Vologda to join the British troops who would be landed in Arkhangelsk, so as to assist them in their advance. This is just a brief summary. You can read more on that.

Lumumba

In 2013, information was made public indicating that the MI6 intelligence service was the mastermind of the assassination (now we are moving to another continent) of Patrice Lumumba, the first democratically elected Prime Minister of the Congo.

A Labour member of the House of Lords said that Baroness Daphne Park of Monmouth had confessed to

The Tipping-Point of History   17

him a few months prior to her death in March 2010 that she had been behind the 1961 assassination of Patrice Lumumba, because she feared that the new democracy would forge an alliance with the Soviet Union.

In a letter to the *London Review of Books*, Lord Lea reported that Daphne Park made her confession as they were having a cup of tea. From 1959 to 1961, she was the Consul and First Secretary to Leopoldville, the capital of the Belgian Congo, which was renamed Kinshasa after the country gained independence. Lord Lea writes, "I mentioned the uproar surrounding Lumumba's abduction and murder, and recalled the theory that MI6 might have had something to do with it. 'We did,' she replied, 'I organized it.' "

Iran 1953

As time went by, official London and its diplomatic missions continued to actively meddle in the domestic affairs of other states and to influence their political regimes.

Suffice it to recall 20th century events when British secret services "took part" in staging a coup d'état in Iran in 1953. Since the early 20th century, British capital controlled the Iranian oil industry via a concession agreement that appropriated most of the country's oil revenues. This situation provoked social and political tensions in Iran, which became more pronounced by the late 1940s and early 1950s. In 1951, Mohammad Mossadegh was appointed Prime Minister of Iran and started implementing an independent foreign and domestic policy. His policies were mostly aimed at eliminating foreign monopolies operating in the country on virtual slave labor terms, to the great detriment of Iranian national interest. The movement for the nationalization of Iranian oilfields became the main symbol of Mossadegh's independent policy.

At that time, oil export revenues were allotted disproportionately in favor of the Anglo-Iranian Oil Company, now called British Petroleum, with British government acting as its main shareholder. With the support of the Majlis (Parliament), Mossadegh passed a law on the nationalization of the Iranian oil industry. This hit British interests hard. After that, official London launched subversive operations against the Iranian government, imposed an international embargo on Iranian petroleum products and thus caused a major economic crisis in Iran.

British diplomats working in Moscow are probably

Former Deputy Fuehrer Rudolf Hess in prison.

listening and recording all this. They will have to send their report to London today. I have done my best, and this statement is 17 pages long. I have one question: Are you proud of your history? Then you need to make a choice: either you advocate human rights, international law and democracy, or you are proud of what you did in the past and continue to do today.

In August 1953, the CIA and the British Secret Intelligence Service staged their joint Operation Ajax to overthrow the government of Mossadegh. A new Iranian government signed another agreement on establishing a consortium of U.S. and British companies that obtained part of Iranian oil revenues and the right to develop oilfields in that country.

British Duplicity Against Its WWII Ally

Although we were members of the Anti-Hitler Coalition, the UK's behavior during World War II can also hardly be called equivocal, due to a number of factors. Some historical episodes give rise to major questions about the essence of the UK's policies on the international scene. This includes, for example, Rudolf Hess' mysterious flight to the UK on the eve of the [1941] German invasion of the Soviet Union. The history of every country has some unpleasant facts, for which future generations will have to pay the price and assume moral responsibility. But the British secret services have classified all the documents on this case for 100 years, and this deadline is being extended.

During the Nuremberg Tribunal, Hess tried to lift the veil of secrecy surrounding his visit, but the British prosecutor, presiding over the court, promptly stopped the hearings. During the break, representatives of British secret services visited Hess, and he later started feigning amnesia. Under the court ruling, Hess was transferred to Spandau Prison to serve a life sentence, but he died there under mysterious circumstances in August 1987, pending his possible release three months later. All relevant documents were classified. The situation remains unclear. Certain facts exist but the full circumstances remain classified.

Volume Five of *Essays on the History of Russian Foreign Intelligence* mentions another extremely curious episode of World War II. A joint British-U.S. plan for a military attack against the Soviet Union was declassified in October 1998 and the relevant files of the UK's National Archives were published. In all, ten German divisions, as well as 47 U.S. and British divisions, were to have attacked the unsuspecting forces of the Soviet Union, then an ally of Washington and London. Intelligence officers received information about Allied military preparations, launched after the surrender of Germany. The plan's codename, Operation Unthinkable, truly reflected its ambitious concept, which involved forcing Soviet Russia to submit to the will of the United States and the British Empire. But, after analyzing the balance of forces and equipment, the new Allies decided that it would prove impossible

Stepan Bandera

Polish citizens being rounded up by British-backed Ukrainian nationalist killers.

to achieve a rapid limited success, and that they would be dragged into a protracted war against superior forces.

OUN and the Murder of Innocents

Another example of subversive operations can be found in Kim Philby's book *My Silent War*, which contains some interesting evidence. In April 1951, London hosted a meeting of representatives of the British and U.S. intelligence services regarding both countries' use of Ukrainian nationalist organizations. Again, everything ties up. By that time, the secret services had supported Stepan Bandera's Organization of Ukrainian Nationalists (OUN) for many years and used them to recruit agents and obtain intelligence on the USSR. Cooperation between OUN and the Intelligence Service grew steadily. In 1949 and 1950, several OUN saboteur squads were parachute-dropped into Ukraine. In the early hours of May 15, 1951, British secret services parachute-dropped three reconnaissance-saboteur squads. Everyone knows about the atrocities committed by Bandera's supporters, including mass executions of civilians, hundreds of thousands of men and women, old people and children, Russians, Ukrainians, Belarusians, Jews, Poles, Czechs, Slovaks and Yugoslavs, the Volhynia massacre, the murder of Polish professors, the Khatyn tragedy, punitive operations in Slovakia, Warsaw and Prague.

British Recruitment of Criminals: Ireland

The British authorities actively recruited professional criminals during their subversive operations. Remember, they told us that Russia is a criminal state with which there should be no cooperation? But the British authorities cooperate nicely with criminals. We are not even talking about White Helmets and people recruited into this organization who are supported all the same.

Let's talk about "mundane" things. In 1973, Her Majesty's Government officially admitted that Kenneth Littlejohn and his brother Keith had robbed banks in the Republic of Ireland for over 12 months in order to discredit the Official Irish Republican Army (IRA). This amounts to classic tactics. Kenneth Littlejohn claims that he was instructed to kill Sean Mac Stíofáin, the former chief of staff of the IRA.

And here is another example: Howard Marx, an Oxford graduate who became a drug dealer, was recruited for the purpose of obtaining information about the IRA's weapons supply chain. In return, the authorities promised not to prosecute him for drug-related crimes. These are isolated examples.

By the way, the British government is known to have created comfortable conditions in the UK for criminals from other countries. According to the UK Home Office's information, for a period between 2005 and 2012, there were over 700 war crime perpetrators living in Britain.

Prisoners

The British authorities also like to use prohibited methods for treating prisoners, especially when they need to get information from them. And, of course, nobody has called off the license to kill.

A recent case in point is the story of Libyan field commander Abdelhakim Belhaj, who was arrested by U.S. special services, after a tip-off from the British, in 2004. After his release in 2009, Belhaj accused London of organizing his abduction and of taking part in his interrogation and torture. He has been fighting for a formal apology from the British government since 2011. He has brought the case against former Foreign Secretary Jack Straw and several MI6 offi-

Abdel Hakim Belhadj

cers, including former Director of Counter-Terrorism Mark Allen, whose correspondence with members of Libya's special services was made public after Muammar Gaddafi's overthrow. We also remember how Gaddafi was removed and that London applauded the execution of the head of a sovereign state.

In December 2013, the High Court of England and Wales concluded that Belhaj's claims cannot be settled in the UK. In July 2016, the Attorney General's Office confirmed its decision to release the MI6 officers involved in the case.

On January 17, 2016, the UK Supreme Court ruled that "claims that the rendition and torture of Abdelhakim Belhaj breached rights enshrined in the Magna Carta should be put before an English court."

It was reported in February 2018 that the next hearing of this case would not be held sooner than 2019. While history is history, claims have been lodged and are being investigated. And the latest news: The Foreign and Commonwealth Office insists that the

Site of the fatal shooting of Zoran Djindjic.

Entrance to Porton Down research park.

hearings be held behind closed doors for national security interests, which is another classical pretext.

In 2015, a non-fiction book titled *The Third Bullet: The Political Background of the Assassination of Zoran Djindjic* was published in Serbia. The authors blame the murder of the Serbian Prime Minister in 2003 on the British intelligence. They claim that the MI6 agent in Serbia, Anthony Monckton, who was connected with the alleged killers, the Zemun criminal clan, was also involved in this crime.

God knows in how many other such cases the UK government is involved. On March 21, 1985, a Soviet engineer working at the Indian nuclear power plant, Valentin Khitrichenko, was assassinated in New Delhi by members of an Afghan terrorist group. What makes us think that the UK special services were involved if Khitrichenko was killed by Afghan terrorists? Those who maintained contact with that group knew about the planned terrorist attack but did nothing to prevent it.

Deaths in UK, Some Related to Porton Down

In conclusion, I will provide the "deadly list" of the prominent and talented people who died a strange death in the UK in the early 21st century.

November 2001: Vladimir Pasechnik, a Soviet microbiologist and former head of the Institute of Highly Pure Biochemical Preparations in Leningrad, dies in Salisbury, allegedly of a stroke. Pasechnik worked at a secret military chemical laboratory at Porton Down. You know about that laboratory at Porton Down. Well, he worked there. While on a trip to France in 1989, he asked for political asylum in the UK and subsequently told the British intelligence service about the alleged biological weapons program in the Soviet Union.

July 2003: a UK authority on biological warfare, David Kelly, was found dead in Oxfordshire. The inquiry [conducted by Lord Hutton] concluded that he had committed suicide. I would like to remind you that David Kelly criticized the Tony Blair government and claimed that the invasion of Iraq in 2003 was based on falsified data. A decade later, the UK government admitted that the data was indeed falsified.

2003: Lawyer Stephen Moss died of a sudden heart attack. He was hired by Boris Berezovsky and his partner Badri Patarkatsishvili to sell the assets of their Devonia investment company.

2004: Dr. Paul Norman, who succeeded David Kelly at the Porton Down laboratory, died in an air crash in Devon. He was a leading chemical and biological weapons expert in the UK.

March 2004: Lawyer Stephen Curtis died in a helicopter crash near Bournemouth Airport. The UK media allege that he feared for his life. Several weeks before his death, he allegedly told his friend, "If anything happens to me in the next few weeks, it will not be an accident." According to the media, Curtis was the managing director of Menatep Group and a lawyer for Boris Berezovsky and Nikolai Glushkov. He was also an independent witness at the hearing of their lawsuit against Forbes in the UK Supreme Court.

More Unexplained Deaths in the UK

Some deaths I will not even mention. Let's just list the major cases.

In November 2006, former officer of the Russian Federal Security Service, Alexander Litvinenko, died in London. I will not go into details, everything is top secret.

In January 2007, one of Yukos' founders, Yury Golubev, died in London.

In February 2008, Badri Patarkatsishvili died of a heart attack in his mansion in Leatherhead, Surrey.

In August 2010, former employee of the Government Communications Headquarters (electronic intelligence), Gareth Williams, died under suspicious circumstances. He was found dead in a sports bag zipped from the outside. Investigators concluded that his death was an accident (allegedly, he got into the bag himself, zipped it and could not get out).

Why are you laughing? This is not funny. This is the official data from the British investigation report.

In April 2012, Richard Holmes, who had worked at a secret military chemical lab in Porton Down, died in Salisbury. The investigation determined that one month before his death, Holmes quit his job for unknown reasons. Forensics found that he died of a stroke. However, his colleagues claimed the scientist had been in great physical shape and had no health problems. Perhaps it has something to do with Porton Down. Maybe it is the toxic environment.

In November 2012, Russian financier Alexander Perepilichny died in Weybridge, Surrey. This case is also very mysterious.

In December 2012, millionaire and real estate tycoon Robert Curtis died in London. According to the investigation, he jumped in front of a train.

In March 2013, Boris Berezovsky died in Ascot. There is nothing to comment on here. Nobody has established what exactly happened there to this day. In December 2014, a close friend of Berezovsky, businessman Scot Young, died in London after he fell out of the fourth floor window. It does happen that people sometimes fall out of the fourth floor windows but it was not the only such death at the time.

In 2016, prominent British scientist and radioactive substance expert Matthew Puncher died in Oxfordshire. He had been a key expert on the Alexander Litvinenko death probe. His death was ruled suicide. Law enforcement agencies promptly closed the case.

The Question of Reputation

I want to say that this smear campaign that the British government is waging against Russia is Britain's stock in trade. This is talking about the reputation at the international scene. And boy, they are constantly talking about our reputation!

I gave you a short list. There are volumes written about what the British government and those who report to it have been doing around the world over centuries, including the 20th and the 21th century. This is nothing new for the people who are aware of this. But the point is that many people are not aware.

Spanish historian Julian Juderias described the British establishment's habit of badmouthing its competitors since the 16th century very well. He gave a definition to this act by the British government ("Black Legend" is a special term used to mean a smear campaign by Britain): "The environment created by the fantastic stories about our homeland that have seen the light of publicity in all countries, the grotesque descriptions that have always been made of the character of Spaniards as individuals and collectively, the denial or at least the systematic ignorance of all that is favorable and beautiful in the various manifestations of culture and art, the accusations that in every era have been flung against Spain" … "which are based on depictions of events that are exaggerated, misinterpreted or indeed entirely false, and finally the claim found in books that at first sight seem respectable and truthful, which is repeatedly reproduced, commentated upon and magnified in the foreign press, that our fatherland should be seen as a lamentable exception among the group of European nations." Once again, this was written by a Spanish historian about the purpose of Black Legend.

But enough of poetry, let's move on to facts. Speaking about the motives suggested by London in the Skripal case and considering the long-standing policy conducted against us by British Ambassador in Russia

Laurie Bristow, it is highly likely that the provocation against the Russian nationals in Salisbury was to the advantage of and perhaps even organized by the British secret services to compromise Russia and its political leadership. Historically, Britain has practiced this on a regular basis. This measure fits in with the general anti-Russian course of the conservative government seeking to demonize our country.

The UK's national security strategy and Prime Minister Theresa May's banquet speech late last year indicate the same.

The outright refusal to cooperate with Russia in the Salisbury poisoning investigation, London's violation of its obligations under the Consular Convention, avoidance of cooperation with the OPCW and concealing source documents essential for an objective investigation are quite illustrative of this.

Grounds for Russian-UK Cooperation?

British officials are constantly quoting from literary classics when they talk to us. During the UN Security Council meeting on April 19, UK Ambassador to the UN, Karen Pierce, mentioned the literary knowledge of Russia's Permanent Representative to the UN, Vasily Nebenzya, noting that she had already decided on a Christmas gift for him saying that she would buy the Russian Ambassador a subscription to the English Literature Club when Christmas comes.

Of course, we are thankful to Ms. Pierce for this interesting idea and, I think, Mr. Nebenzya, too, will find the right words when he speaks at the UN Security Council next time. As you may be aware, we never leave a favor unanswered. Why wait another eight months for the New Year or Christmas to arrive? We can see what difficulties the British government is running into when it comes to history based on a statement made by British Ambassador to Russia Laurie Bristow.

Recently we signed an agreement on cooperation with the Russian Military History Society. In this regard, we can put in a word for Ms. Pierce and the entire British government to have them accepted as honorary members of the Russian Military History Society. This status will not only provide them access to the Society's vast archives, but also allow them to take part in developing key areas of scientific research in the field of history. That'll give us a chance to at least work together.

South Africa's Zuma Indicts British Empire in TV Address

April 22—South African leader Jacob Zuma exposed the long history of British imperial warfare against the people of South Africa, in an hour-long address to a "Blacks in Dialogue" event in Braamfontein, Johannesburg on April 21. It was carried live by ANN7 television and then posted on the ANN7 website. Zuma's public attack on the British is unprecedented in South Africa. The event was sponsored by Black First Land First (BLF).

The theme of former President Zuma's address was the need for political unity to get Black majority control of the economy, especially the land. Zuma spent the first 30 minutes just on the British wars, massacres, and punitive expeditions against South Africans throughout the 19th century, which only ended in 1906, when the British machine-gunned 800 Zulus trapped in the Mome Gorge in the Bambatha Rebellion. Between 3,000 and 4,000 Africans died at the hands of the British in that 1906 war alone. Zuma went on to note the exclusion of Africans from any role in government and administration when the Union of South Africa was formed in 1910, and the continuing dispossession of Africans' land thereafter.

He stated that the British also could not accept the existence of the two Afrikaner republics, the Zuid-Afrikaansche Republiek of Paul Kruger and the Oranje Vrijstaat, which led to British aggression in the two Anglo-Boer wars.

Zuma called for expropriation, without compensation, of the land seized under the 1913 Native Land Act, which then left Black Africans with only 7% of the land for 80% the country's population.

The leader of LaRouche South Africa, R.P. Tsokolibane, has long specified that the President of South Africa must sustain a public attack on the British Empire to enable the people of the country to understand what is holding South Africa down.

The video: http://www.ann7.com/former-president-jacob-zuma-speaks-of-the-injustices-of-land-dispossession/

American Poverty and Its Solution

by Robert Ingraham

April 21—On April 7, 2018, following her presentation to a Schiller Institute conference in New York City, Helga Zepp-LaRouche was asked the following,

Question: My question is, how do we overcome this violence? How do we overcome this culture of death, and how do we overcome this culture of violence? And more importantly, how do we stop getting young people wanting to escape

discussed is the imperative to eliminate poverty entirely, and to do this now. The reality of day-to-day poverty for tens of millions Americans is either ignored or seen as a problem to be "managed." There are many government programs to help the poor and disadvantaged, and some of them are laudatory. Yet the numbers of poor continue to rise, and these programs, by themselves, will not prevent this. Poverty is usually discussed—in the media, government reports, and news

maniopisfoundation.org

Homeless family.

USDA/Lance Cheung

A couple leaving a local food pantry supplied by the U.S. Dept. of Agriculture.

CC/Consumerist Dot Com Follow

Low-wage, no future, job at a McDonald's fast food restaurant.

from reality by taking drugs and whatnot? So that's my question.

Zepp-LaRouche: I think what we need for that is a mass movement for development.

The subject of this report is poverty. In this, the second decade of the 21st Century, the magnitude of the crisis of poverty in the United States is a subject that is not fully grasped by many foreign observers, and it is one that is little addressed in a serious manner by American news media and elected officials. What is never

articles—as a matter of statistics, of numbers on a spreadsheet. Slight changes in these numbers, or minuscule motion in one direction or another are often trumpeted as evidence of the success or failure of current governmental economic policy.

But we are not dealing with statistics. We are dealing with human beings—tens of millions of men, women and children who live year in and year out in conditions of horrific poverty, with no remedy in sight. The societal and cultural effect of this reality is destroying the future of the nation.

One of the most devastating products of permanent widespread poverty is the effect it has had on the youth of the nation. With many consigned to minimum wage jobs—at best—with no productive future in sight, and with no purpose to their lives, millions of youth have become entrapped in the oppressive neotenous world of drug usage and dead-end hedonism. This is precisely the desired scenario prescribed by H.G. Wells a century ago.

In this report, we shall examine two aspects of this crisis. First, a look at the actual state of poverty in the United States, including the effects of such poverty on the morale and morality of the American people. Second, we will examine the need to Think Big in regard to what needs to be done—the need to get away from "managing poverty," or at best achieving incremental improvements in poverty reduction, and to look toward the bolder mission of eradicating poverty entirely.

I. Defending the People

There was a time in the recent history of the United States—say 1944 to 1963 (or perhaps 1971)—when the economic mission of America was primarily a global one. Domestically, America was moving forward; new technologies, new scientific breakthroughs and rational credit policies were advancing the conditions of life for the American people, and despite setbacks such as the 1957-1958 recession, an upward thrust in both living standards and national productivity was a reality. During those years, many thoughtful individuals recognized that the proper role for America was to follow through on the anti-colonial post-World War II perspective of Franklin Roosevelt to marshal the awesome physical-economic might of America to accomplish a world-wide economic revolution—to use the same methods which had created the Tennessee Valley Authority to transform and uplift the economies of the former British, Dutch and French colonies worldwide.

This is no longer the situation today. Since 1971, and escalating dramatically after 1987, we have witnessed the widespread destruction of America's economic capabilities. The magnificent scientific/industrial engine which served the nation—beginning really from 1936-38, through to 1971 is no more. America is primarily a formerly industrialized nation, and the impact of that policy of deindustrialization—driven by financial policies originating in the City of London—

has been catastrophic. Today, it is the American people who need rescuing. The economic destruction of America has produced devastating effects on the livelihoods and physical existence of the nation's citizens, but far greater damage has been done to souls of Americans. Where optimism vanishes and despair flourishes, civilization itself is in jeopardy. This defines the mission of our times.

This is not to argue that America must "turn inward." This is not a question of either/or. It is simply to recognize the enormity of the task which must be accomplished here. Today, a powerful dynamic has been unleashed in the world through the Belt and Road Initiative, led by China and its partners. A future of profound global economic transformation is opening before us. Yet, the leadership of China, themselves, have clearly recognized their own responsibility to uplift the conditions of life for their own people. At the same time that China is now aggressively pursuing a path of global economic development through the Belt and Road Initiative and related projects, that nation is also in its fourth decade of an effort to eradicate poverty within its own boundaries. A commitment to the "Peoples' Livelihood" begins with one's own people. We see, under both Xi Jinping as well as Vladimir Putin, an unshakable moral commitment to advance the conditions of life for the people in their respective nations. Such is urgently required in America.

Poverty in America: the Current Reality

According to the U.S. Census Bureau, 12.7 percent of the American people—or 43.1 million people—live below the official poverty line. Given the fact that this is greater than the entire population of California, that figure alone is alarming. Yet it is only the tip of the iceberg.

The U.S. government defines poverty as a yearly income of less than $12,060 for an individual, $16,240 for a couple, and $24,600 for a family of four. Such figures are murderously absurd. Anyone living at such a level is not merely poor; they are in danger of starvation. It should be noted that the Census Bureau has a sub-category called "deep poverty," which means a household income below 50 percent of the poverty threshold, i.e., less than $12,300 for a family of four. According to the Census Bureau, in 2017 18.5 million people reported deep poverty.

There is a second category defined as "near poverty," i.e., those whose income is between 100 percent and 125 percent of the official poverty cut-off line. This would include, for example, a family of four whose income is between $24,601 and $29,104. According to Census figures, there are 14.7 million people now living in "near poverty."

Many have called for a redefinition of the term "near poverty," to increase its range to those individuals and households whose income is between 100 percent and 150 percent of the official poverty rate (i.e., up to $34,500 for a family of four). If we were to use this broader definition of "near poverty," the number of people living in "near poverty" jumps to 30 million. So, if you take the official number of people in poverty—43.1 million—and add those whose income goes up to 150 percent of the official poverty rate—30 million—you end up with 73.1 million, or 22.4 percent of the U.S. population—larger than the entire population of France.

Of course, the Jesuitical term "near poverty" is a fraud. All of these 73.1 million people are poor. Their lives are merely defined by their level of misery and desperation as the income figures go down.

But there is more.

Others who have studied the issue of poverty have proposed a term "Economic insecurity" for those families whose household income is less than $42,000 per year. Forty-five percent of all Americans (147 million people), including *fifty-six percent of all children,* fall below that income figure. These 147 million people are everywhere. A large percentage live in the suburbs. Almost 30 percent of them hold down full time jobs.

It should also be noted that the number of Americans living in "economic insecurity" is going up. From 2007 to 2012 it has risen from 37 percent to 45 percent among the total population, and for children it has risen from 47 percent to 56 percent.

As stunning as these figures are, one also has to consider the nearly 29 million households (25.4 percent of the population) making between $42,000 and $75,000. These are often households where the husband and wife, between them, are working three or four jobs, just to pay the bills. Family life is destroyed; children are left unsupervised; and the societal damage is enormous. (I am personally acquainted with a Mexican-American chef, who also works a second job as a janitor, for a combined 90 hours a week, to support his family. His wife also works a full-time 40 hour per week job.)

The figures for black Americans and other minorities are significantly worse. Additionally, probably the hardest hit by poverty are households headed by unmarried or divorced women. Female-led households have a combined poverty and near-poverty rate of almost 40 percent.

Wages

With the evaporation of high-wage skilled labor during the last thirty years, a nightmare has been created where to escape from poverty has become near impossible. The current U.S. minimum wage is $7.25 per hour, which for a full-time forty-hour per week job comes out to a yearly income of $15,080. Some states and cities have implemented a higher minimum wage, including California, Massachusetts and New York, but this tends to occur in areas where the cost of living is substantially higher than the national average, thus offsetting the additional income.

During the last five years, more than half of all the new jobs created in America were low-wage jobs, either at the minimum wage or slightly higher. According to the National Employment Law Project, 42.4 percent of American workers currently make less than $15 an hour. And those 42.4 percent also support millions of children and other non-working household members. The vast majority of the jobs held by these individuals are in the realm of unskilled and semi-skilled labor. The American workforce and American culture has been decimated.

There are many in America, particularly on the political "left" who are lobbying intensively for raising the federal minimum wage. This, however, is no panacea. Take the case of Richmond, California. Its local minimum wage of $13 per hour is among the highest in the nation, yet it is an impoverished city, with high unemployment, and suffering from the presence of violent drug gangs and widespread drug addiction. Yes, the purchasing power of the American citizen must be increased, and no one should work for $7.25 per hour or $9.25 per hour or even $11.25 per hour, but approaching this crisis by simply demanding an increase in the minimum wage will not accomplish what is actually required.

Murdering the Future

The purpose of citing all of these statistics is not so that you, the reader will wring your hands, or "shed a tear" for the poor. What is required is to think about the future, about the continued advancement of human civ-

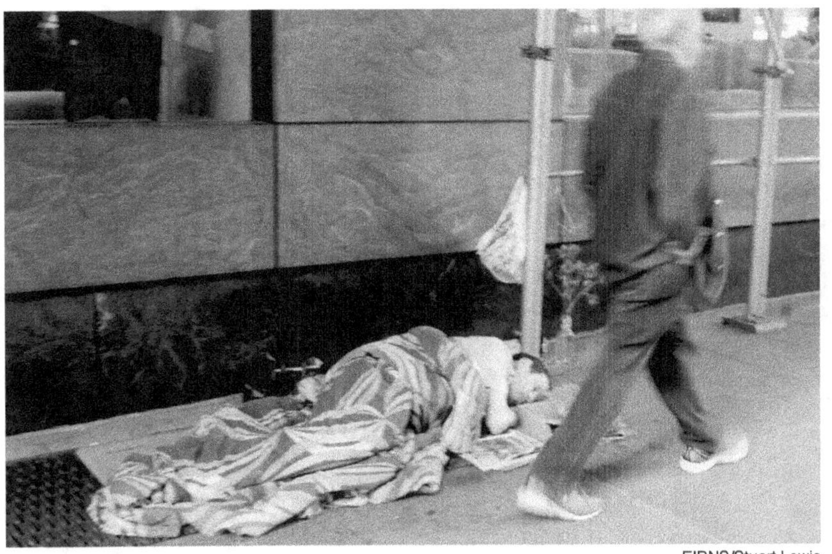

Do we ignore the homeless when we walk past them?

ilization. Consider this: According to "Feeding America," there are 41 million households in the U.S. that suffer from food insecurity and 13 million of those have children in them. A 2013 UNICEF report ranked the U.S. as having the second highest relative child poverty rates in the developed world. Children living in poverty are more likely to have learning disabilities or developmental delays, which means they aren't as prepared for primary school. They have higher rates of absenteeism or just drop out altogether. By 4th grade, students from low-income households are already an average of 2 years behind grade level. High school students living in poverty or low-income households are seven times more likely to drop out of school than those coming from higher-income households. Children who grow up in poverty are also more likely to have children when they're still teenagers, or to be incarcerated.

According to a report issued by the Economic Policy Institute in 2016, youth unemployment for high school graduates stands at 33.8 percent for whites, 51.3 percent for blacks and 36.1 percent for Hispanics. It is far worse for those who have not completed high school. At the same time, it is now reported by the Centers for Disease Control that one out of fifteen Americans is now addicted to heroin or some other opioid. That's 20 million Americans who are addicted. And these figures do not include consumption of methamphetamines, hallucinogens, ecstasy, or other "designer" drugs. Again, the use and addiction to these drugs is heavily concentrated among the younger age groups. This most precious resource of the nation, a resource which fore-

tells the future nation's potential, is being killed off.

As of 2014, 1.36 million public school students were homeless in America. This figure is up ten percent from 2012. In New York City, the number of homeless public school students jumped to 145,239 in 2017, a figure greater than the total population of the State Capital at Albany, and one in every seven New York City public school students will be homeless at some point during elementary school. At the Mott Haven Academy Charter school in the Bronx, two-thirds of the students are in the child welfare system. This crisis is not restricted to New York or the large American cities. Such conditions exist in every state from Maine to California.

The acceptance of permanent poverty—and wide income disparity—has a second victim, beyond those who are most obviously affected. Pessimism and despair throughout the entire population are the byproducts of such an entropic process. Ask yourself this: What is the moral effect on individuals in American cities who, on their way to work each morning, have to step over homeless persons sleeping on the sidewalk, or who are dunned in their cars at every red light by a homeless person for a contribution? Such an environment pounds at the senses; it eats away at the soul. It generates an indifferent callousness. The acceptance of such human suffering, and the personal failure on a daily basis to do anything about it, makes every individual morally smaller. It causes one's heart to shrink. Every member of society is reduced to a Hobbesian individual. There is nothing left that binds us together in common cause.

In 2015, an estimated 2.7 million Americans were evicted from their residences, with the highest rate of evictions occurring in Memphis, Phoenix, Atlanta, and Indianapolis. In 2012, there were 29,000 evictions in New York City. That's 80 evictions per day, every day. In Milwaukee, a city of fewer than 105,000 renter households, landlords evict roughly 16,000 adults and children each year. Several studies have shown that such evictions often lead to a worsening downward spiral into poverty. Today, the majority of poor renting families in America spend over half of their income on housing, and at least one in four dedicates over 70 per-

Homeless camp near Laney College in Oakland, CA.

cent of their income to paying the rent and keeping the lights on. This nationwide crisis has been powerfully documented by Matthew Desmond in his 2012 book, *Evicted: Poverty and Profit in the American City.*

In November of 2016, the author of this report published, in *EIR,* an article on poverty and homelessness, including the appearance of "tent cities," in Oakland California. In the eighteen months since that article was published, the crisis has grown exponentially worse. What were, at that time, scattered tent city communities have now grown to dozens, if not hundreds, of tent city camps in every part of the city, some of which have grown to the size of city blocks, containing 50 to 100 tents, where the residents have erected outer walls of plywood and other debris to mark the boundary of their "city." Reportedly, the situation in Los Angeles County is even worse. It is also clear that this is now a national phenomenon.

II. Think Big

On September 8, 2009, Lyndon LaRouche delivered a speech in Washington, DC, where he stated the following:

> We're dealing with a demoralization of the U.S. population, which is losing confidence in itself, and confidence in the future. This is what we have to concentrate on.
>
> We have to create real employment. Not employment in make-work, but real employment in some kind of productive work, the way Roosevelt did, in the Depression years, in the beginning. We have to put people back to work. We don't have the work for them? Yes, we have to provide unemployment compensation, to keep them alive and keep them in condition. And keep their dignity, above all. We've got to save communities, which are no longer productive, put them back into productivity. We're going to concentrate largely on basic economic infrastructure, physical infrastructure of the type that's necessary for the foundation of industry.
>
> Now, when you build large-scale infrastructure programs, you also create a lot of private employment. Because, when you have a major contract, a government contract, for building a piece of infrastructure, what do you do? You call in private firms as bidders on contracts, to service the completion of this work. In that way, wherever you put in a transportation project, for example, or some other project which is a government project, you immediately stimulate employment, of this type, in the vicinity. People who have skills, who have small businesses or something, or that kind of skill, who can bid on the job, or do that job—we've got to do that, fast.
>
> The first thing we have to do, is to do enough of it, to convince the people out there, that that's what we intend to do. Think back to the experience, as I saw it, and others saw it, back in the 1930s. The first thing to do: You've got to rebuild the confidence of those people out there, who are feeling desperate, in themselves. You've got to rebuild confidence in those communities which are affected by the desolation which is being caused now.

You've got to create productive employment, Mr. President! Not green employment! Productive employment! You have to fix up the Ohio River, which is no longer functioning, because of neglect. You've got to fix up the Mississippi River; you've got to build up the Missouri River! You've got to build up the Ogallala Aquifer, in the West, if you want agriculture for the future. There are many things to do: Get cracking at it! Pick a few of these projects, get them started! Correlate the way you start these projects, with the way you locate revitalization of employment in industries and local communities. As we used to do.

Look at a map of the United States: Go state by state, cooperate with the state officials, map the problem. Decide where you need the social effect of employment. And find the form of employment that fits the program, and make sure they get a share of it there. We want to have an increase, by about 20 percent, of employment of the people of the United States, over the immediate period ahead. We want them to feel that that is a Christmas present, and a New Year's greeting, for a change in the way things are going! The American people are trusting, and if you show respect for them, and respect for their needs, and a sense of justice, they will trust you for a certain period of time.

This 2009 call by Lyndon LaRouche is the only rational place to start toward rebuilding the American economy and restoring hope and morality to the American people. Anything else is off topic.

Since the election of Donald Trump in November, 2016, there has been a great deal of discussion concerning rebuilding American infrastructure. Much of it is incompetent. All of it is inadequate. What are being put forward are limited, small approaches, very few of which will have a dramatic effect on increasing national productivity, and the sum total of what is being pro-

Eroded hillside and damaged spillway in Oroville, CA in 2017.

posed utterly fails to address the urgent national requirements 50 to 100 years into the future. Everyone is thinking too small. Additionally, the projects and proposals being bandied about—were they all built—will have a negligible impact on reducing the poverty which is destroying the lives of tens of millions.

Infrastructure

Take the case of the American Society of Civil Engineers (ASCE), an organization which, to its credit, has kept alive a serious discussion about the infrastructure investment required for the nation. In its 2017 report, the ASCE estimates that the United States needs $2.2 trillion dollars of infrastructure spending during the next five years and $4.6 trillion by 2025 to bring U.S. infrastructure to an "acceptable standard." They point to the horrendous conditions of American bridges, dams, roads and water systems. On a scale of A to F, the ASCE rates U.S. infrastructure as D+.

The average age of the 90,000 dams in the United States is 56 years. By 2025, seven out of ten of them will be more than half a century old. The country has 15,500 "high-hazard potential dams," meaning that loss of life would be probable if they failed. More than 640,000 miles of high-voltage electric lines are at full capacity. Most U.S. power lines were constructed in the

1950s and 1960s and are already past their life expectancy. Public transit is also "chronically underfunded," ASCE says, and airport infrastructure and air traffic control systems are "not keeping up."

Here is where the problem in thinking arises. Almost all of the $2.2 trillion which the ASCE proposes to spend in the next five years—with no serious proposal as to where that money will come from outside of new taxes and fees—is intended to merely avert catastrophe, i.e., to repair and replace already existing—but obsolete—infrastructure. While necessary, this does not even come close to providing for future productive growth, nor will it have any significant effect on reducing the poverty and suffering of the American people. It is merely a start, and a very inadequate one at that.

One example of the fallacy of thinking inherent in the ASCE proposals can be seen in their 2017 Infrastructure Report Card, which grades the nation's roads a "D," bridges a "C+," transit a "D-," and aviation infrastructure a "D." Yet it rates America's railroads a "B," this because the railroads are meeting current demands, and the more profitable freight lines have continued to repair and maintain their roadbeds, rails and other equipment. But America has zero miles of true high-speed lines, while China has built over 16,000 miles of high speed rail, with many of the trains routinely traveling at speeds of over 200 mph. Long distance rail passenger traffic has almost disappeared in America, while in China 672 million rail trips were taken in 2013 and over 2.9 billion passengers have taken a high-speed train trip between April, 2007 and October, 2014. China is thinking toward the future, while America is trying to stave off collapse.

While it is true that the larger figure of $4.6 trillion, which the ASCE proposes should be invested in infrastructure by 2025, does include a few new projects that will benefit the nation, this is still far, far too little.

Conduct an experiment. Get in a car and drive across America. Make sure to visit as many "inner city" communities in the nation's urban areas as is possible—e.g., Baltimore, Detroit, Philadelphia, Chicago. Don't pass up the tens of thousands of small rural communities either. Get out of your car on Halstead Street in Chicago, Livernois Avenue in Detroit, or Prospect Street in Indianapolis. Walk around. Talk to some of the local inhabitants. And, most important, observe carefully what you see. Mass poverty, from coast to coast. Unskilled, largely poorly educated, and despairing citizens are the norm, not the exception. And there are even more rural poor than urban—millions of individuals scattered throughout thousands of small and medium sized communities across the country. Additionally, some of the worst poverty is to be found in "suburbia," in the medium-sized communities and cities of formerly productive regions.

Thousands of square miles, including large sections of the Bronx and Brooklyn, need to be completely rebuilt. So-called "soft infrastructure," such as schools, public hospitals, libraries and senior housing will themselves alone require a massive investment.

Our orientation—the only sane orientation—is not to adopt an "acceptable standard." Our goal must be—not to "manage" poverty, not simply to replace old infrastructure with new, not to create marginal physical economic growth. Our unshakable goal must be to eradicate poverty and build for the future.

III. Hamilton's Solution

The escape route out of our current national nightmare is to be found in the mind of Alexander Hamilton. America was founded on the economic approach invented by Hamilton, and its happiest and most prosperous times were when the nation adhered to his precepts. In this section we shall examine the two post-Washington Presidencies—those of Abraham Lincoln and Franklin Roosevelt—when such a Hamiltonian approach was most successful. (Although it was abbreviated, a legitimate case could be made to include John Fitzgerald Kennedy's creation of the manned moon mission as a third successful case.)

This examination will be brief, almost cursory, out of necessity. The magnificent initiatives and programs of those two Presidencies will not be addressed here in any serious depth. What is presented here is not a recipe. It merely gives a flavor to what great initiatives have accomplished in the past. In truth, if we are to meet the challenges of today, we will be required to go beyond what Roosevelt and Lincoln accomplished.

In 1933 Franklin Roosevelt launched the unprecedented Tennessee Valley Authority (TVA) project. At the same time he also created both the Civilian Conservation Corps (CCC) and the Federal Emergency Relief Administration (FERA), which together rescued seven million unemployed Americans—mostly young—and gave them jobs. Later, he would also

Tennessee Valley Authority (TVA) power line installation, part of Franklin Roosevelt's "New Deal" rural electrification.

President Franklin Roosevelt at the Boulder Dam, 1935.

Civilian Conservation Corps (CCC) Camp BR-24 Boise Project, Marsing, Idaho.

Works Progress Administration (WPA) construction.

create both the Civil Works Administration (CWA) and the Works Progress Administration (WPA), the latter of which employed an additional eight million, three million of whom were hired in its first year of operation.

Between 1933 and 1935, through both direct and indirect employment, FERA created more than twenty million jobs, the equivalent today of forty-five million jobs. Initially, some of these were "make work" jobs, simply designed to stave off starvation and get people back into the labor force. But if one looks at the CWA, for example, CWA workers laid twelve million feet of sewer pipe, and built or made substantial improvements to 255,000 miles of roads, 40,000 schools, and nearly 1,000 airports. The CWA also paid to put 50,000 teachers back to work. Under FERA, the CWA, the CCC, and the WPA, more than 14,000 new schools were built, as were 1,000 new public libraries; 12,000 road projects were carried out, and more than 120,000 new buildings, including post offices, courthouses, firehouses and armories, were constructed.

The great Four Corners projects transformed the energy, fresh water and transportation infrastructure of the nation, profoundly advancing the productive potential of the Republic. Additionally, the Public Works Administration (PWA) constructed the Grand Coulee Dam, the Bonneville Dam, the Triborough Bridge, the Lincoln Tunnel, LaGuardia Airport, Los Angeles Airport, and the Upper Mississippi River locks and dams. There were hundreds of such projects. Rural electrification was carried out, leading to the general electrification of the entire nation.

With the Tennessee Valley Authority, Franklin Roosevelt took a region, including parts of seven states and encompassing an area eighty percent the size of England, and utterly transformed it, utilizing the most advanced industrial, technological and scientific means available at that time. The region in question was the poorest in the nation, with only a small fraction of the residents having access to electricity. Income for many families was below $100 per year. Under the slogan of "electricity for all," more than forty-five dams and hydro-electric projects were built. Additionally, more than twenty coal-fired and natural gas power plants were constructed. A region of the nation, one which encompasses 80,000 square miles, was profoundly upgraded.

Financing the Miracle

Between 1933 and 1935 the Federal Emergency Relief Administration and the Public Works Administration together spent $9.1 billion on infrastructure

U.S. Bureau of Reclamation

Grand Coulee Dam, one of President Franklin Roosevelt's projects.

cc/Patrick Handrigan

LaGuardia Airport in New York City.

construction. That represented 15.9 percent of the nation's Gross Domestic Product (GDP). An equivalent expenditure for today's GDP would be $3.0 trillion. And that $9.1 billion figure was only what was spent by FERA and the PWA; it does not include any of the additional spending by the WPA, the CCC, the NYA, or several other agencies active in the first years of the

New Deal. It also does not include the vast sums spent on the TVA, nor the massive credit made available through the Reconstruction Finance Corporation (RFC) or the reorganized commercial banking system.

The RFC was a quasi-public corporation. Its initial capital came from $500 million in stock sold to the U.S. Treasury. The RFC raised an additional $1.5 billion by selling bonds to the Treasury, which the Treasury in turn sold to the public. In the years that followed, the RFC borrowed an additional $51.3 billion from the Treasury and $3.1 billion directly from the public. All of these obligations were guaranteed by the federal government.

This combined borrowing by the RFC of $55.9 billion is a dollar amount almost equivalent to the nation's 1933 Gross Domestic Product of $57 billion.

Although it was originally intended as a vehicle to provide financial relief for banks, a July, 1932 amendment to the RFC charter authorized the RFC to loan funds to state and municipal governments. Once Franklin Roosevelt was in office, the RFC was directed to use this enhanced power to provide loans for infrastructure projects, such as the construction of dams and bridges. The loans could also fund relief for the unemployed, as long as repayment was guaranteed by tax receipts. The RFC became the largest generator of credit in the nation.

At the same time, the Roosevelt Presidency enacted Glass-Steagall and also implemented several other laws to eliminate various forms of financial speculation. The financial resources of the nation were harnessed, using the Hamiltonian power of the U.S. Treasury, to finance a great economic recovery.

Abraham Lincoln

Between 1861 and 1865, Abraham Lincoln implemented a series of revolutionary economic and banking measures. First, he used the sovereign power of the United States to issue more than $400 million in paper currency (legal tender "Greenbacks") directly from the U.S. Treasury. Additionally, through his ally, Jay Cooke, the Treasury sold $1.3 billion of so-called 5:20 government bonds (redeemable in 5 years, reaching maturity in 20 years)—not to foreign bankers, but directly to the American public. Other bonds were sold as well, bringing the total issuance of new federal credit to well over $2 billion, about 50 percent of the GDP of the Union states.

At the same time, large amounts of the new Greenbacks were loaned to the member banks of the newly created National Banking System. Held on deposit by those banks, these Greenbacks served as the security for the banks to begin issuing loans for the many and varied economic projects carried out under the Lincoln Presidency. A conveyor belt of Credit—essentially a U.S. Treasury-led National Credit System—was created.

It is true that much of this money went into financing the Union's war effort, but also consider that—both during the Lincoln Presidency and in the years that followed—U.S. railroad mileage went from 45,000 to 157,000, more than in all of Europe. Entire new industries were created. American steel production and modern American agriculture were unique in the world.

In considering the magnitude of what was accomplished under both Lincoln and FDR, it must also be recognized that their breakthroughs took place under very adverse conditions. The entirety of the Lincoln Presidency took place during wartime, in which the defeat of the South took precedence over all other considerations. FDR suffered from not having a National Bank and having to operate within a hostile world fi-

Mathew Brady Studio/Thomas Le Mere

Abraham Lincoln, 1863.

nancial system controlled from London. Today, were the United States to revisit the approach of Lincoln and FDR, while simultaneously joining with China, Russia and other nations in the cooperative Belt and Road Initiative, accomplishments of wonderment, barely imaginable, become possible.

There are No Limits to Growth

At this point, it is essential to make a critical observation. We can admire and learn much from the examples of Franklin Roosevelt, Abraham Lincoln and John Kennedy, but the mistake we should not make is to limit ourselves to the great things that they were able to accomplish, nor to the policies they implemented. We can go beyond FDR, Lincoln and JFK, and we can accomplish much more.

In 1972, Jay Forrester and Dennis and Donella Meadows, of the Club of Rome, published their fraudulent Malthusian argument, *The Limits to Growth*, wherein they argued that there is a natural limit on the physical development of human society. This was merely one initiative in the post-1971 British Empire effort to extinguish scientific and technological optimism in Europe and America.

Today, there is another type of Limits to Growth, a mental box which inhibits the thinking about economic and financial policy. Many individuals insist that there exists, essentially, a "financial" limit to growth, i.e., that there are axiomatic financial boundaries which constrain—and even prohibit—a rapid upward development of the human condition.

It is critical to defeat this mental pathology. Various government officials in Washington DC talk about spending $1 trillion dollars, or less, on the nation's infrastructure. The ASCE proposes to spend $4.6 trillion by 2025. In financing his great economic development projects, Franklin Roosevelt, through both direct government spending and federally-backed credit, spent a dollar amount more than 100 percent of the nation's GDP. Today that would be roughly $19 trillion. Why can't we spend that? Why can't we spend more than that? Might it not pe possible to even spend double that? What Lincoln and FDR did are the shining heroic examples, but they are not the limit!

It comes down to people thinking through what the proper roles for the U.S. Treasury, our banking system, and our National Credit System should be. What is their purpose? Why do they exist? And, most important, how can the full mighty resources of this potential Credit System be mobilized to the full extent of its power—straining all bounds, as we did during World War II—to completely eradicate poverty and create an entirely new future society?

This can be done. Learn from FDR and Lincoln, *and then go beyond them to even greater accomplishments*. The great projects they built are not the limit. The methods they utilized to deploy Public Credit to finance these projects are also not a limit. A National Credit System, particularly as it has been re-defined by Lyndon LaRouche, can be a creature of awesome, almost unimaginable, power. What is required is a war-time mentality to carry out a full economic mobilization. Every resource must be utilized.

Such an economic recovery can not proceed stepwise or linearly—building bricks one on top of another. We begin with the possibility of where we need to be in 100 years. From there, we define the key transformative interventions which need to be made; and from there develop a Bill of Materials for what is needed. Start from the future. Start from the top. Solve the key problems. The future necessary potential drives the steps to be taken today.

Given the nature of the universe, we will never know perfectly where we need to be a century hence, but we can define certain necessary goals, and we can operate on the basis of a clear directionality. Those goals and that directionality will also demand certain "leaps" in comprehending and implementing new "platforms" of increased human productivity, with a focus on the most challenging scientific problems.

The axiomatic approach must be to build for two generations out, while keeping an eye on the longer range needs for a century or more into the future. Any perspective to "replace or repair" existing infrastructure must be abandoned. We must build for the requirements of increasingly prosperous future generations.

Pressing Needs

Our first action, however, must be to rescue the people. Evictions and foreclosures must stop. Food security for every individual must be secured. Jobs and job training must recruit millions. Tangible, visible progress must become apparent to everyone in the nation. All of this has to be done, and it must be accomplished at the same time we take on the larger, grander projects which the nation urgently requires.

IV. Us or Them: Kill Off the British Empire

Attentive readers of *EIR* may observe that an article authored by Paul Gallagher in last week's issue contains material directly relevant to the subject under discussion here. That article, a review of the documentary film *The Spider's Web: Britain's Second Empire,* reveals, at least by implication, the approach required to ensure success for a policy of economic development.

Since 1987, the British elites have succeeded in establishing (or re-establishing) the City of London as the de facto controller—one might

Stock market big-board display.

even say dictator—over trans-Atlantic financial and banking markets. As the film establishes, the City sits at the center of a vast global network of unregulated "offshore" banks located primarily in British overseas territories, such as the Cayman Islands. Today, 25 percent of the world's financial activity, and 50 percent of financial derivatives betting, is conducted on British territory. Three-quarters of the world's hedge funds are registered in the Caymans alone. By 1997, 90 percent of all international loans were already being made in the "Euromarket," centered in London.

The U.S. banking sector has largely been swallowed up by this London-centered Colossus, and in reality it is fallacious to even speak today about a "sovereign" U.S. banking system. By 2014, the biggest U.S. banks held almost 70 percent of their on and off-balance sheet foreign assets in London. This surrender of independence by U.S. banks has also been accompanied by a massive growth in their financial assets. By December 2011, the assets of America's five largest banks' were equal to 56 percent of the U.S. economy, compared with 43 percent only five years earlier.

These catastrophic developments were greatly exacerbated by the repeal of Glass- Steagall, with the Gramm-Leach-Bliley Act in 1999, and related actions to legalize over- the-counter derivatives trading and other forms of parasitical financial speculation.

Lessons to be Drawn

Three things to consider:

The first—and bitter—reality to be faced is that over the last three decades, the City of London and their subservient pals on Wall Street have succeeded in creating a near- monopoly over international banking and credit in the trans-Atlantic world. Only the new dynamic of the Belt and Road Initiative is outside their grasp. Their overriding priority has been to maximize fictitious monetary profits. At the same time, credit for productive investment—worldwide—has simply been choked off. In Europe, nations lie supine beneath the heel of Brussels and the European Central Bank. In the United States, no elected official dares to propose a sovereign U.S. banking and credit policy, and the nation's urgent physical needs go begging. For the nations of Africa and Ibero-America it is even worse. Paltry loans are doled out for the most minuscule of projects by the London creditors, and then only under the most brutal conditionalities. Meanwhile, what available domestic credit exists in those poor nations becomes the victim of "capital flight," to the tune of $1 trillion per year, with most of that going to London banks and their related "offshore" jurisdictions, there to be funneled into the machine of financial speculation.

A second matter to consider, however, is that the seeds to solving a great crisis are often to be found within the crisis itself. If one looks at the magnitude of the London-based financial octopus—including the U.S. financial assets parked there—this can also be viewed as a great resource for accomplishing global economic development. It is true that much of this monetary "wealth"—such as financial derivatives and the activities of the hedge funds—is nothing but imaginary monopoly money that will have to be written off, but that will still leave trillions of dollars in financial assets which, under a serious Hamiltonian approach, could be put to productive use. As stated earlier, ask yourself: What is the purpose of a banking system? Why does it exist? Properly understood and properly managed—under the direction of the U.S. Treasury—existing American bank assets could be deployed to play a major role in the rebuilding of the nation.

The third and final consideration in this section is to recognize that this three-decade effort by London to enforce its will on the nations of the world is now crumbling, and a new economic and financial reality is spreading throughout the world as a result of the Chinese-led Belt and Road Initiative. Through the Hamiltonian approach of its own banking system, as well as through institutions such as the Asian Infrastructure Investment Bank (AIIB), China is now leading a global campaign to invest huge sums into infrastructure and other physical-economic projects world-wide. Although this endeavor has only been underway for a handful of years, the results already are astonishing, and they are a sign of the end of British imperial financial domination. Hope is spreading to nations throughout the planet.

Were the United States to adopt an economic/financial approach coherent with the Chinese initiatives, victory would be all but guaranteed. The first step must be to re- impose Franklin Roosevelt's Glass-Steagall legislation. That one action—alone—would force U.S. banks to sever their financial assets from the City of London and abandon the bulk of their speculative financial practices. More will have to be done, but that is the necessary starting point, and such an action would produce profound consequences.

There is one additional benefit to ending the era of British financial speculation which must be mentioned here. There are infrastructure projects being built today in America, but in case after case, these projects have run up against the roadblock of exorbitant costs. For example, while nominal infrastructure spending on water and transportation increased from $277 billion in 2003 to $335 billion in 2007, real infrastructure spend-

Chinese Vice Premier Deng Xiaoping (center) with President Jimmy Carter. Deng Xiaoping began China's reform and opening up policy in the 1970s.

ing fell by $24 billion, or 6.3%, during the same time period because of the rising costs of commodities such as petroleum, iron, and gravel. What we are witnessing here is the product of unbridled financial speculation in the raw materials markets by London and off-shore speculators. The price of numerous commodities, as well as the price of real estate has been speculatively driven up way beyond what these commodities are actually worth. Kill the speculative beast, and sanity shall return to much of these matters.

V. Building the Unknown Global Future

American leftists of the Saul Alinsky variety used to enjoy repeating, *ad nauseam,* the pop phrase "Think globally but act locally." In the situation within which we find ourselves today, one way to think about a way to move forward, a way to resolve the current crisis, is to reverse that recipe: "Think locally, but act Globally." We must not shrink from confronting the profound economic and societal crisis which grips America. We can not afford to ignore it. Massive rebuilding is required. Yet, the economic solution, the path to reconstruction, will only succeed if the United States links up with Russia, China and other nations of good will to put an end to the dictatorial power of the City of London once and for all. London's grip over finance, credit and banking must end. Cooperating sovereign nations must forge a new international system of Public Credit for investment in those great projects which will rescue both America and the entire world. Alexander Hamilton would smile at this prospect.

China's War on Poverty

In the forty years since the initiation of China's "reform and opening up" policy by Deng Xiaoping, somewhere between 700 and 800 millions of Chinese people have been lifted out of poverty. Most London-allied western commentators have made light of this or poked jabs at it, but clearly nothing even close to this has ever before been achieved in human history.

Xinhua photo

China has lifted 700 million people out of poverty. President Xi Jinping greets people in Jinggangshan City in 2016.

Today, much attention is given to the massive investments made by the Chinese in their physical economy, including high-speed rail, subway systems, power plants, water management, port development, the computer and related electronics industry, as well as the escalating Chinese commitment to space exploration. Such attention is well-placed, and should serve as a model for what should be done in the United States and nations all over the world. However, there is another, less noticed, side to what the Chinese have done.

The Chinese have initiated an in-depth effort to directly help the people of their nation. Under the Special Nationwide Poverty Reduction Policies and Programs, numerous anti-poverty organizations and agencies have been created, each with its own mandate. These include the State Council Leading Group on Poverty Alleviation, the State Council Poverty Alleviation Office, Provincial Poverty Alleviation Offices, Provincial Leading Groups on Poverty Alleviation, Prefecture Poverty Alleviation Offices, Prefecture Leading Groups on Poverty Alleviation, County Leading Groups on Poverty Alleviation, County Poverty Alleviation Offices, and Township Poverty Reduction Staffs. These agencies serve as both a top-to-bottom and bottom-to-top multi-faceted machine to identify and remedy conditions of poverty, from the inner city to the tiniest of rural villages.

The goal is to achieve common prosperity and harmonious development and to eliminate poverty entirely.

Many programs and local initiatives have been tested and tried. In the case of urban poverty, which has been largely eliminated—take note New York and Los Angeles—this has been done through direct government payments to poor urban dwellers, bringing their income up to a minimum level of 4,476 yuan per month ($700 at an international exchange rate). In some ways these efforts echo the relief programs of the Roosevelt Administration, but in terms of the breadth and depth of what the Chinese have done, there really is no precedent.

There is no dichotomy between what the Chinese have accomplished domestically and the initiatives they are now taking globally. The intention, the operational philosophy of the two are seamless. British and Anglo-American mouthpieces accuse China of geopolitical designs in Africa and elsewhere, but the proof that these are lies is given by what China has done to honor and uplift its own people, governed by a "win-win" outlook, which also forms the basis for the great development projects they are now helping to build, even among some of the poorest nations.

As Saint Paul stated "And now there remain faith, hope, and charity, these three: but the greatest of these is charity." More than one hundred years ago, Sun Yat-sen enunciated his "Three Principles of the People." Of these, the greatest is the third, Minsheng, the People's Livelihood. This is where one must start in any rational, moral discussion of economic policy.

Kenya's New Mega-Infrastructure, the Mombasa-Nairobi Railway

by P.D. Lawton

P.D. Lawton, born in South Africa, is a member of Solidarité & progrès, the LaRouche movement in France. She is a researcher and writer on African affairs. This article is reprinted, with editing, from her website, African Agenda (English-language).

April 14—Amazing and wonderful things are happening all across Africa, as that continent begins a giant leap into a modernized incredible future! China is investing in African infrastructure at an astonishing rate, bringing the African nations into the New Paradigm and 'Win-Win' spirit of China's Belt and Road Initiative. By issuing credit for the construction of mega-infrastructure, China

Xinhua/Chen Cheng

The first passenger train of the Mombasa-Nairobi Standard Gauge Railway arrives in Nairobi, May 31, 2017. A video overview of the project is "My Railway, My Story— Documentary about Mombasa-Nairobi Railway," https://youtu.be/p9Z0eYHWFCl

is assisting African nations to invest in the future, investments based on the development of Africa's physical economy! We are so fortunate to be alive in these times and to be able to witness the continent's transformation with mega-development projects which will free the human creativity of Africa's people and provide them with an economic renaissance.

The Mombasa-Nairobi Standard Gauge Railway (SGR) is the largest, most expensive infrastructure project ever undertaken in Kenya. Its 480 km of super modern construction traverses mountain ranges, wetlands and national parks. The project has found innovative solutions to a multitude of social, environmental and geographic problems in its journey from the Indian Ocean port of Mombasa directly into the interior of East Africa and Kenya's thriving capital, Nai-

robi, home to over 4 million people. Mombasa is the largest sea port in East Africa and is its key trade gateway.

The old railway from Mombasa to Nairobi is over 100 years old and it could only carry 1 million tons of freight each year. The main highway is in poor condition and parts are severely over-crowded. Up until now the old railway and the motorway have been Kenyans' only direct path between the coast and the interior. As the old railway deteriorated over the decades, the Rift Valley Railway Consortium of Kenya and Uganda reported losses of $1.5 million in 2014.

In 2009 the Kenyan government agreed to work with the China Road and Bridge Corporation to construct a standard gauge railway from Mombasa to Nairobi. Work commenced in December 2014. China's

Xinhua/Chen Cheng

Mombasa-Nairobi railway in Kenya.

Exim Bank has extended credit for 90% of the project. By May 2016, initial track laying was completed in just over 1 year. Passenger service was opened May 31, 2017, an astounding eighteen months ahead of schedule! Freight services commenced in January 2018.

The journey time between the two cities has been reduced from ten to four hours. It now takes less than half the time to travel the nearly 500 km—incredible! The economic advantages of reducing travel time and improving access between the port of Mombasa and Nairobi are immeasurable. This constitutes a qualitative improvement of the Kenyan economy, an advancement that will transform the economy beyond all previous limits. In a few years' time it will become obvious that the $3.8 billion cost of this mega-infrastructure project will seem like nothing compared to the vast improvements it will make in developing the physical economy by building the country's infrastructure, an incalculably sound investment in the future! Infrastructure is the key element of the physical economy without which manufacturing cannot develop.

Proof of Principle

Not only will the Mombasa-Nairobi Railway transform Kenya's economy, it is also the first part of the Belt and Road Initiative's Northern Corridor Integration Project (NCIP). It is the primary section of a planned series of railways to connect the Great Lakes region to the Indian Ocean. This is only the beginning of the radical economic transformation of not just Kenya, but also Burundi, Rwanda, Uganda, Democratic Republic of Congo (DRC) and also South Sudan. Through mega-infrastructure projects such as this and the Transaqua Project, the African interior will be transformed through economic development. As proven by the construction of the Mombasa-Nairobi Railroad, mega-infrastructure does not have to destroy ecosystems and national parks, all these things can be creatively designed in such a way that they can symbolize a dialogue and communion between man and nature and actually enhance the wellbeing of both humans and the natural kingdom.

The Mombasa-Nairobi railway has provided 60 jobs per kilometer of line. More than 30,000 Kenyans are now employed including highly skilled professionals.

Ninety percent of the total railway workforce is

Xinhua

Track-laying machine at work on Mombasa-Nairobi railway.

Mombasa-Nairobi railway, women drivers being trained.

Xinhua/Sun Ruibo

Kenyan, including many women who have been selected on ability and are now working in various occupations, from site engineers to project supervisors and even plant operators—and they are loving it! There are also eight women train drivers who are part of a team trained in China in the operation of the highly sophisticated locomotives. This is a hugely positive human investment. The SGR train drivers were selected on the basis of ability and their passion for the project.

Factories were built along the route of the railway to make the required parts. Rail ties are used for support and transmission. These factories can make 1400 concrete ties per day as well as colossal steel T-beams weighing 143 tons each! On-site production increases efficiency, provides local employment and drastically reduces the overall production time.

Each section of track is composed of 44 rail ties spanning 25 meters and weighing 15 tons. It takes just 4 minutes to lay a track panel. There is a margin of error of less than 2 cm, and with perfect precision the railway fits together like a jigsaw puzzle! Seventy-nine bridges grace the course of the railway. The Ormagerigara Bridge is a colossal 807.46 m long.

The making of high-performance concrete for rail and bridge construction requires an ingredient called coal ash, also known as fly ash. Kenya has always had to import its fly ash. As demand for concrete was outstripping supply, the China Academy of Construction Research came up with a solution. They proposed using volcanic ash instead of fly ash. As Kenya is situated on the Great Rift Valley, it is abundant in volcanic ash, especially in the area near Nairobi. Tests showed that volcanic ash was a perfect substitute for fly ash. This is a fantastic discovery that solved an immediate problem, reduced the costs, boosted local production, invented a new industry, helped the Kenyan government from having to import fly ash, and provides a solution for all the countries on the Great Rift Valley of East Africa with an essential ingredient for construction and infrastructure. Wider applications will be found and who knows what else this discovery will bring. Amazing!

The railway passes through Tsavo National Park, which is the largest wildlife reserve in Kenya, which currently relies heavily on tourism. Tsavo covers more than 13,000 square kilometers and at its widest point is 240 km across. This ecosystem has around 13,000-14,000 elephants, a much loved and respected animal in Kenya and the world. When the railway was first pro-

Xinhua/Sun Ruibo

Zebra leaving an animal passageway of the Mombasa-Nairobi railway in Kenya.

posed, environmentalist groups strongly objected to it on the grounds that it would destroy the natural beauty of the environment and disrupt and disturb the local populations of many species such as elephant, wildebeest and rhino.

The Kenyan Wildlife Department was very concerned about the potential negative impact. China, however, had encountered similar problems in their own national parks and ecosystems. Drawing on years of experience, Prof. Zhang Jingqiao, who is the project designer of the Mombasa-Nairobi Railway, was able to apply extraordinary measures based on China's past experiences to incorporate the needs of the local wildlife into the design and construction of the line. Similar problems were encountered in China when constructing the Qianghai Tibet Railway that traverses a particularly beautiful wilderness, home of the endangered Tibetan antelope. Thirty-three wildlife passages were built along the line, and over the past ten years the migratory animals have become perfectly accustomed to using these manmade corridors. This solution has been applied in Kenya and is proving to already be a success. Lions, elephants and migratory herds are all beginning to use the 14 corridors which are either bridges or culverts traversing the railway! Vast sections of the railway that cross Tsavo have been elevated on beautifully designed viaducts, leaving the wildlife completely unaffected!

Emali is a town of 25,000 residents that has been bisected by the railway. The movement of cattle is important to the lives of many from Emali, and the railway has created a problem for them. Another concern was that the line would separate the town's two schools. The railway project's community liaison officer discussed all these problems with the residents and proposed a pedestrian bridge to cross the line. The $2 million bridge had not been factored into the initial cost, but the Chinese project manager for that section of the line said that the additional cost was a worthy investment because it made the children's lives safer. Within a month of the decision to build, the 700 ton steel bridge was

Pedestrian bridge near the Emali station of the Mombasa-Nairobi railway. It has been designed so that it can also be used as a livestock overpass.

completed and has reduced the children's daily walking distance by 3 km. The bridge has also been designed so that it can safely be used by livestock as well as pedestrians.

Think Now of Transaqua

The Mombasa-Nairobi Railway is proof that mega-infrastructure is a plus-plus investment; there are no negatives; the project only brings benefits. With creative solutions it is possible to overcome any and all obstacles, be they social, environmental or geographic. The lives of millions of people are being enhanced by investment in mega-infrastructure and the physical economy. With the Mombasa-Nairobi Railway as working proof of this principle, surely the wider public can now see that the Transaqua Project can become the single most important investment in the futures of millions upon millions of people in Africa. Kenya's mega-infrastructure is proof that we do not need to destroy the environment in order to develop. Transaqua has the potential to completely rewrite the history of the African interior and to transform the livelihoods and economies of all 12 participating nations.

Africa is on the brink of the most incredible future, working in conjunction with China's Belt and Road Initiative and the New Silk Road. Development plans of amazing creativity can change the course of history, not just for Africans but for the entire world.

Unlocking the Secrets of the Aurorae

by Janet G. West

April 20—Cave paintings in France, dating to 30,000 years ago, reveal to us that prehistoric man was in awe of what we now call the Aurora Borealis, or Northern Lights. This eerie and beautiful phenomenon is, in fact, a near-Earth laboratory in which we can study the profoundly non-empty nature of space. Since the dawn of mankind, we have pondered the firmament and have sought to understand the nonvisible causes of the rhythms of the heavens. Thousands of years of scientific inquiry and experimentation have not only enabled us to navigate the oceans, but have encouraged us to explore our Solar system and beyond.

Frederic Church's 1865 painting of Aurora Borealis.

On February 27, 2018, NASA released more information on the "Grand Challenge Initiative-Cusp" (CGI-Cusp), a two-year mission to investigate the upper reaches of the atmosphere and the regions home to the Aurorae—the Northern Lights (*Aurora Borealis*) and the Southern Lights (*Aurora Australis*). An international team of researchers and scientists will study the results of a series of launches of sub-orbital sounding rockets from two sites in Norway into the magnetosphere. According to NASA, GGI-Cusp will "investigate the physics of heating and charged particle precipitation in this region called the geomagnetic cusp—one of the few places on Earth with easy access to the electrically charged solar wind that pervades the Solar system." Planning for the project began in 2012.

NASA also reports that, "Understanding the contribution that auroras make to the total amount of energy that enters and leaves Earth's geospace system—referred to as auroral forcing—is one of the major goals of the NASA-funded Auroral Zone Upwelling Rocket Experiment, or AZURE. The more we learn about auroras, the more we understand about the fundamental processes that drive near-Earth space."

Some of the launches will release chemical tracers that will allow scientists to create a 3-D image of the flow of particles through the ionosphere (similar to a wind tunnel); others will track the flow of charged particles during their flight. This is an electrifying commencement for a total of eleven launches and eight missions, and should open the door for discoveries.

The Aurorae were extensively reported in Ancient Greece, before the time of Plato. Anders Celsius, in 1741, noted the connection between the Northern Lights and magnetic activity. In 1743, the great 18th Century Russian scientist, Mikhail Lomonosov, began a series of scientific studies of the Northern Lights. The science of geophysics, and the developments pioneered in the 1800s by Carl Friedrich Gauss, opened the way to the study of the characteristics of the magnetosphere.

The study of any phenomenon in the cosmos naturally involves electromagnetic fields, and the Aurorae are no exception. Some among you may now be asking, "Why study these areas?" or "Why is this important *now*?"

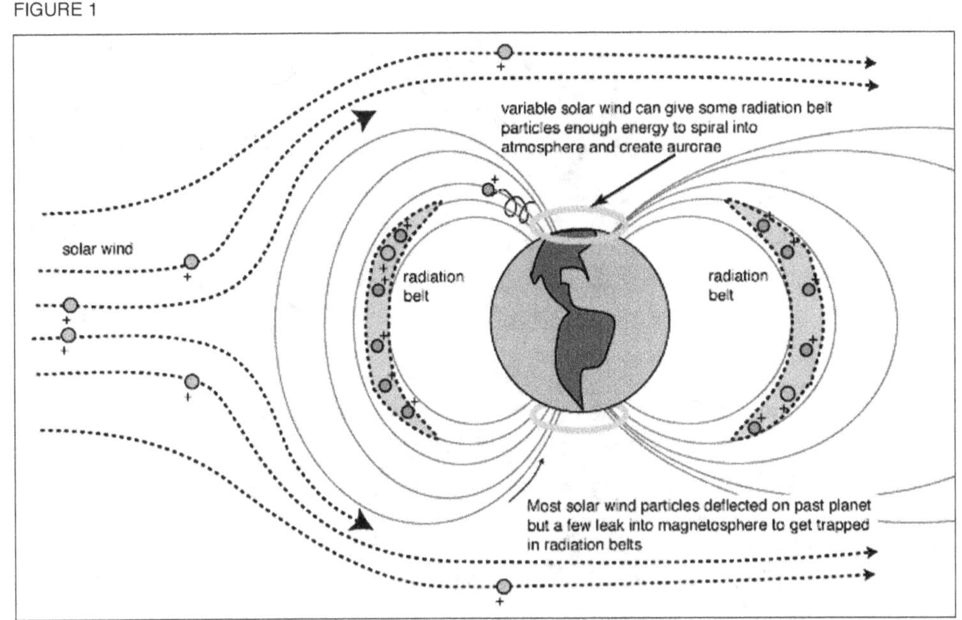

Earth's 'Halos'

If you're at least as smart as a caveman, then your mind won't be fooled into believing what your senses are telling you. One of the major challenges to colonization of other planets, is the impact of cosmic radiation on human beings. Much of our modern technology—especially the miniaturization of computers and some medical devices—is thanks to the tremendous spin-offs and discoveries from the mission to land man on the Moon, as conceived by President John F. Kennedy. The in-depth study of the Aurorae will create breakthroughs in our understanding of the universe, and will help us create technologies to explore and develop the universe, on Earth and beyond.

The Aurorae are a result of a complex cascade of reactions between the Sun and the Earth's electromagnetic fields. The Sun is constantly emitting high energy particles and radiation that reach Earth's magnetic field as a "solar wind." Some particles, captured in the field, are funneled to the two poles, known as the "magnetic cusp."[1] These streams of high-energy particles then impact and interact with the mole-cules of gases in the upper atmosphere, emitting visible light when the energized electrons fall back to lower energy levels; the different colors we see generally have to do with the type of gases impacted: oxygen generates yellows and greens; nitrogen generates reds, blues and violets (**Figure 1**).

Aurora activity correlates with the occurrence of sunspots on our Sun, which follow a roughly 11-year cycle. Strong solar activity has been linked to widespread interference with the electrical grid in northern latitudes.

Although the general physics of how the Aurorae are generated is mostly understood, it has been remarkably difficult for scientists to forecast changes in the Aurorae due to activity in the processes of the heliosphere and magnetosphere.

In recent years, there has been broad international cooperation among many nations for the study of the Aurorae, with studies too numerous to detail here. Of note are a research center in Iceland, funded by China and shaped like a ship and pointing northward (**Figure 2**),[2] and the array of three identical satellites launched

2. https://karholl.is/en/

1. Recent missions have shown that the solar wind pressure is decreasing. The impact of this change is still under study. See: https://science.nasa.gov/science-news/science-at-nasa/2008/23sep_solarwind

FIGURE 2

Northern Lights and Upper Atmosphere Observatory in Karholl, Iceland.

by the European Space Agency (ESA) to observe events in Earth's magnetosphere, called SWARM.[3]

Aurorae Singularities

Although Aurorae are remarkable in and of themselves, they are most interesting when they "misbehave." Contrary to their appearance as "peaceful" and "enchanting," they represent powerful and dynamic forces. And, far from being in "empty space," the environs of Earth and beyond can only be understood as Lyndon LaRouche describes: "Recently accumulated investigations bearing on the leading role of what is termed a 'cosmic radiation' permeating what is never, and nowhere a part of 'empty space,' now depend on deeper insight into the conclusive quality and forward-looking implications of the apparent qualitative divisions, and interrelations among the lithosphere, biosphere, and noösphere within the confines of that region which our Solar system inhabits on our galaxy's periphery."[4]

In the mid-1950s, scientists discovered a new type of activity generated by geomagnetic storms, which was barely visible to the naked eye, since it was in the red wavelength range.[5] It was a sub-visual emission that was picked up by a photometer. The scientists were surprised by the fact that it was stable for about 24 hours, and appeared much further south than the familiar aurora arc; it was dubbed a Stable Aurora Red (SAR) arc. The scientists noted, "While aurorae come from impulsive bursts of energetic particles along high-latitude magnetic field lines (and therefore from distant regions in the magnetosphere), SAR arcs come from a prolonged drainage of heat from the Van Allen radiation belt regions that move closer to Earth during large geomagnetic storms. Hence, SAR arcs occur at mid-latitudes."[6] An alliance of several space agencies was formed, along with many hundreds of citizen-scientists, who continue to research the SAR arc. A photo of a SAR arc was captured in 2016 by Scottish amateur astronomer and photographer Stewart Watt.[7]

CC/Elfie Hall

STEVE image captured at Little Bow Resort, Alberta, Canada.

The most striking feature of this activity is that though the arc is generally stable, it twists and spirals upwards, indicating the presence of a vortex of more concentrated energies. This should remind one of the twisted filaments observed in a controlled thermonuclear fusion reaction. If these energies could somehow be harnessed, what kind of reaction would occur, and how could it serve mankind?

In 2017, thanks to the SWARM mission, supersonic plasma jets high in our atmosphere were discovered; these are known as "Birkeland Currents," first postulated about a century ago by Norwegian scientist Kristian Birkeland.[8] Although still being re-

---

3. "Introducing SWARM" https://www.esa.int/Our_Activities/Observing_the_Earth/Swarm/Introducing_Swarm

4. "The Death of London's Roman Empire," *EIR* Feb. 3, 2017, p. 49.

5. The human visual range is narrow; it is difficult to focus on objects close to the infrared range, as well as the blue/ultraviolet range ("black light"). Red light allows the eye to function in near-darkness, hence its use on submarines and some auto dashboards.

6. "A Stable Auroral Arc Over Europe," *Astronomy & Geophysics*, Volume 53, Issue 1, February 1, 2012, pp. 1.16-1.18, https://academic.oup.com/astrogeo/article/53/1/1.16/218252

7. See: https://www.dailyrecord.co.uk/scotland-now/mysterious-proton-arc-aurora-spotted-8989150

8. "Supersonic Plasma Jets Discovered." https://www.esa.int/Our_Activities/Observing_the_Earth/Swarm/Supersonic_plasma_jets_discovered

Strong Thermal Emission Velocity Enhancement (STEVE) aurora.

searched, these huge sheets of energy are believed to carry about 1 terawatt of electrical power—about 30 times more than what New York City uses during a heat wave.

Most stunning, however, has been the recent discovery of yet another type of auroral arc, which was captured on film in 2017 by an amateur scientist in Calgary, Canada. This unfamiliar activity was dubbed a "Strong Thermal Emission Velocity Enhancement" (STEVE).

Unlike the shimmering curtains of light of the Aurorae, STEVE is a stable arc aligned East-West across the sky, at lower latitude than the Northern Lights. It appears whitish to the eye, but shows up purple on camera, lasting around 30 minutes, with short-lived green "fingers" lying perpendicular to the main arc (**Figure 3**). STEVE is of such great interest that NASA has set up a task force called Aurorasaurus, appealing to citizen-scientists around the globe to participate in further research.[9]

The Creative Spark

Each step forward in science always brings new questions and potential, and often takes the path of a sailing ship tacking into the wind. To look ahead to the colonization of the Solar system and beyond, mankind must begin to master the underlying physical principles of celestial electromagnetic fields and find ways in which their energy may be harnessed; the Aurorae offer a perfect laboratory right in our own "backyard." You, the reader, can play a role in this great endeavor—by placing yourself in history, studying the great scientific minds of history, and becoming a citizen-scientist. Now is the time to shift humanity into a new, culturally optimistic paradigm!

Let this beautiful global phenomenon serve to unite mankind in a peaceful and fruitful exploration of our Solar system and beyond.

For Further Information

The National Oceanic and Atmospheric Administration (NOAA) has an online map that shows auroral activity in 30-minute increments: https://www.swpc.noaa.gov/products/aurora-30-minute-forecast

To join the search for STEVE: https://www.nasa.gov/feature/goddard/2018/mystery-of-purple-lights-in-sky-solved-with-help-from-citizen-scientists

---

9. "Canadian Amateurs Discover a New Type of Aurora." Includes excellent video clips. https://www.theatlantic.com/science/archive/2018/03/amateur-scientists-discover-a-new-type-of-aurora/555491/

December 9, 2013

SCIENCE & MORALITY …

Science & the Solar System

by Lyndon H. LaRouche, Jr.

The subject which I present here, pertains from the start, specifically, to a particular form of abuse against students, one which many educational institutions have continued to practice, throughout the course of my experience, from that of being a student, to, later, as a professional. The commonplace error which I have experienced on both accounts, over the course of that part of my actual lifetime experiences, has been my view of a consideration of the unfortunate effects, which I have often witnessed, not only upon witnessing the commonplace errors, but as the just cause for my response to the usually bad effects of the inherent failures of what passes, in almost any generation, as a standard education.

That error, in both the earlier and later roles of the educational process within our United States which I had experienced, for me, had been based on a false presumption as to the definition of "truth," as I have experienced that issue in that education which I had confronted, first, as a student, and, later, as a professional in a certain branch of science. In both domains, the quality of performance which I had experienced in both states of affairs, has been, usually, merely conditional at its best, that for reason of a heretofore presently "standardized," but erroneous popular presumption respecting the appropriate intention of the educational process. The quality of performance, as I had witnessed in either sets of situations, has been marginal at best, and, on balance, has been declining at an accelerating rate, since the murdered post-John F. Kennedy's 1960s.

Therefore:

The root and outcome of the folly of most practiced

education on that account, is to have been properly attributed, chiefly, to the effect of limiting the definition of "truth" to the effects of certain prevalent practices of what has been considered as a customary education, but also the result of a commonly misguided standard for the practice of an "education" rooted in what are actually pathetic presumptions respecting the nature of the human mind. Unfortunately, that standard has thus been, typically, the fallacious presumption which has been, either explicitly, or, otherwise implicitly, that the students are to be graded, more or less, according to the measure of their conformity with prescribed facts of a standard of merely (academically) alleged truth, which is thus a discouraging, even a punishing experience, in one way or another; thus, a legacy of students who actually fail in the subsequent course of life, for reason of their accepting such a prescribed, ostensibly a-priori instruction.

A typical proof of such a currently, increasingly frequent, academically abusive use of the educational system, is to be shown by what the student should have received, instead, which should have been required for the student, for students whose future training must be in the domain of physical science and its branches, but who, instead, had been, typically, inclined to submit to such hoaxes as the folly named Euclidean Geometry, or worse.

The same evil has been widely responsible for the quality of evil which defines the global outreach of the world's oligarchical system, a practice which has been, generally, efficiently typified by the succession of those imperial Anglo-Dutch oligarchies' reductionists' styles. Those and their likeness now, who are still presently operating today under the guidance of such intentions, are still under the same general category of such nakedly imperialistic reductionists as Adam Smith and Jeremy Bentham, no more than two centuries or so later. I am referring to a particular category to be identified as the heritage of those Anglo-Dutch, oligarchical "reductionists" who are best recognized in the history of notoriety, for their having been traced in European history to much earlier origins in such circumstances as the genocide applied against the people of Troy. That is to be recognized as what had been also familiar to that region's history since such as ancient Rome, through to the presently Anglo-Dutch imperial tyranny which is currently infesting the financial practice of our own United States.

That history has been an association with a currently avowed commitment to an intended reduction of the current human population, a reduction as from about seven billions persons on this planet recently, to no more than a single billion (as according to the Queen of England) in our immediate future. Its characteristic has been a mode of genocide which, I emphasize again, as having been, typically, perpetrated, earlier, against the population of the ancient city of Troy. It is a tradition which is continued to the present date, still continued in the guise of the particular aspect of the U.S.A.'s "Anglo-Dutch" imperial interest, as it may be known to much of the world, as the pollution which is "Wall Street."

The evil which that aforesaid moment of history represents, still to the present date, has often been manifest to the relevant observer, essentially, as the expression of an account of history which is identified as of the

The folly of most modern education, writes LaRouche, is "a commonly misguided standard for the practice of an 'education' rooted in what are actually pathetic presumptions respecting the nature of the human mind." Shown: Goya, Capricho 37, "Might not the pupil know more?" (1797-98).

"oligarchical principle," a practice of monetarists, or by like parasites, which is, chiefly, widely commonplace as imposed among much of the notable branches of the education of the human species, to the present date. It is a practice of parasitism which has been continued, as under such names as "Wall Street" and London; but is guided, under various titles, throughout much of the history of this planet, still to the present moments.

This following set of the facts reported here, as also others which are often products of the same intention, is what we are obliged to define, once more, as an approach to the presently most crucial issues of actually physical principle, which are posed, for example, by what now includes the threats from such as both asteroids and comets. However, on this occasion, rather than focusing on those particular objects as such, I shall now, here below, stress a view of such subject-matters as those, considered from the essential vantage-point of a critical view of the functions of the human mind as such, as mind is distinct, in its true meaning, from mere sense-perception.

I. Soul & Body: The Enigma

The principles of science which I reference hereinafter, will have been relatively long and large in their making, often even long before they had been represented in print.

At their root, the basis of the principles in which my own discoveries are currently relevant, has earned my displeasure with any chosen literal basis in merely mathematics *per se*. My essential commitment, as it is still today, has been active contempt for the commonplace practice of the application of reductionist ideologies to living social processes; this includes the category of human behavior in its biological expression as essentially a subject of the human mind (rather than the reductionists' notion of merely the brain), and, hence, also of what is truly Classical drama in all its relevant aspects of scientific and Classical-artistic expressions.

It was against that background, that I had begun a certain special series of written drafts and published works during the middle to late 1990s; this had led, in turn, but much down the line, to several drafts and published pieces leading into the piece titled as my June 10, 2013 **Nicholas of Cusa, Kepler & Shakespeare**.[1] It has been against that background that most of my recent discoveries on this account have come forward, subsequently, through to the present time.

My argument here reflects my continued treatments of that same matter of principle.

The Present State of These Affairs

The commonplace presumptions, those which I will have rejected here, below, as having been functionally silly, or worse, are, in one sense, also commonplace practices, often also academic standards, but are, also, a collection of a numerous, essentially incompetent, shallow set of presumptions which have been customarily adopted as established authorities. These are presumptions which continue, more or less, to be spread as among popular and even scientific and related institutions presently, that often done with a great deal of feigned, and sometimes very pompous solemnity.

Such misguided presumptions as those, typify the particular cult-doctrine which demands popular faith in even mere sense-perception as such, which it is demanded must be accepted as even a virtually physical standard of academic fustian, and, also, actually, that of an attempted replacement for an entirely different metric: an honestly, practically principled test of truth-

Despite the achievements of the Renaissance and later scientific advances, such as those in astronomy, "the evidence is, that the obscene cult of sense-certainty, has largely still persisted." Shown: Johannes Vermeer, "The Astronomer" (ca. 1668).

ful regard for personal integrity.[2] As an example for such popular misbehavior, to which I have already referred here, we should consider the inclusion of such failures by those who insisted, on a similar basis for the customary follies of "popular opinion:" even the medieval opinion that the world is, even still today, not very far from an essentially "Flat Earth" idea of space and society, as that runs according to a large amount of present presumptions concerning society.

After we had considered the work of truly modern scientific geniuses, such as the relevant, most notable, earlier modern geniuses Filippo Brunelleschi and Nicholas of Cusa in the Renaissance, and the work of Cusa's scientific heir, Johannes Kepler; we mean such as those of the latter pair, Cusa and Kepler, who had laid the foundations of those physical principles of astronomy,

---

1. EIR, June 21, 2013 or LaRouchePAC.

2. This means the rejection of such frauds as faith in sense-perception as such, as I shall clarify that in progress, at a later point here.

on which the development of an actually modern physical science had depended: then, the particular nonsense popular in the earlier Medieval interval, had been since, hopefully, largely discarded among serious thinkers to the present date.

Nonetheless, despite the earlier achievements and later frustrations of the Renaissance, the evidence is, that the obscene cult of sense-certainty, has largely still persisted. Sense-certainty is, indeed, still an ugly cult, as I shall emphasize the notable facts in the following pages. We must show here, why this has been so into present times. Consider the following.

Back to 'Genesis'?

In fact, it is to be argued here, that, in retrospect, the most important principle presently known to mankind, should be now recognized as being the truly universal principle of the same notion of Creation attributed to the most remarkably exceptional precision of the exhaustively serious first chapter of the book of **Genesis**. Both the Solar system and the Galaxy, are among the crucial items of what should be considered as related evidence: those notions bearing on the spoor and the concept of creation, are that on which the notions of those entities and their processes depend for their justified respect by the human observer. The particular fact is, that the first Chapter of **Genesis** is as close to a principle of truth, such as the notion of the existence of a provable notion of "mortal man," as we might require for our source of a broad notion of certainty at this moment of our considerations here, as I shall show that below.

However, there are, otherwise, what might seem, mistakenly, to some persons to be plausible exceptions to my foregoing statements. Their opinion has been contrary to the evidence of the evolution of, implicitly, all other species, excepting, particularly, the uniqueness of the principles expressed by the voluntary factor in the evolution of the human species, a species which has been an exception to the cases met among all alternative, presently known living species.

Next to the most important feature in this portrait which I have suggested here, there is the manifest evidence of the qualitatively superior quality of the "creative power" (i.e., the actualized *noëtic* powers of the developed member of the human species). However, it is most important (for the sake of completeness), that only "the quality of the mind-process of the human species," affords the members of our species the uniquely willful ability to create the effectively higher, self-evolutionary abilities unique to the potentials of the human mind. These are powers associated uniquely with our species, thus reflecting certain unique powers not shared by any other known form of animal life: those powers of the human mind which are not shared by any other kind of living species presently known, by us, to exist.

However, most among the members of the human species, as known from what have been estimated as "earliest" relevant times, are known to the present stocks of persons associated with contemporary historical times; but, even those have developed the manifest qualifications of the human species in respect to what should be regarded as that species' most significant respects. Sample achievements of relatively higher energy-flux densities, will probably never reach fully the highest levels ultimately accessible to mankind.

In the meanwhile, most humans have been kept in an inferior, more-or-less nearer-to-bestial state of mind than what I am willing to treat as acceptable as a standard for humanity presently; that short-fall has been indicated to have been the effect of a social process of suppression of the role of human creativity, a failure which is to be attributed, essentially, to the long-term domination of the human species by the category of what is to be identified, historically, as the oligarchical system; that has been, and remains, a system signifying those followers of the frankly satanic Zeus (i.e., "the prototype of the oligarchical system"): I mean Zeus-followers who have been the adversaries of the cause of "mankind the fire-bringer," which latter is another categorical name for Prometheus.

Since Very Ancient Greece

The immediately preceding references to ancient Greek legends, are, in fact, in no way merely pointing to what were merely legends.

The identification of the Ancient Greeks' legendary Zeus-versus-Prometheus conflict, like their named echoes, and those of their mutual enemies, such as the Aristotle (and Euclid) who has been the opponent of Plato, are not so much mythical figures, as "meta-historically" actual ones. In particular, the difference between the beast and the human personality, is identified by, and embodied in the role of the human being, whenever man is otherwise to be known in generic history as

Prometheus committed the sin of loving mankind, giving him fire (science), from which man would learn many arts, and hope (for the future), for which he was to be tortured by Zeus for eternity, as depicted in this ca. 555 B.C. painting on a Laconian kylix (drinking cup).

"The Fire Bringer," as opposed to the cases of the beast who does not rely upon a mankind-controlled development willingly.[3] Those two contrasted types, bestial versus truly human, may merely appear to represent parallel cases, as with an implied heredity in respect to a relatively unique affinity to either Cain (**Zeus**), or Abel (**Prometheus**), respectively. When the latter pair of figures from presumed mythological origins, are examined for the distinctions of the violent beast from the uniquely fire-using human, the consequence of those compared usages is the distinction of the differences of the characteristics of mankind from the (oligarchically) systemically cruel beast.

The comparisons which I have just introduced here, do indeed fit the evil of the oligarchical system, as opposed to the human nobility of man-as-the-fire-bringer. The systemic features of the counterposed types, are systemically defined as respectively adversaries. The image of the mass-murders of the Christians in the Roman arenas (for example), is consistent with the principled characteristics of the thus-counterposed pro-Satanic types.[4]

---

3. I.e., the case of man-controlled animal.
4. The distinction between the two types is systemic, not particular.

Mankind as a Spiritual Entity Per Se

Now, juxtapose that just-stated view which I had portrayed above, with the thesis which I have presented in a series of developments of this theme in my already indicated work, published as **Nicholas of Cusa, Kepler & Shakespeare** of June 10, 2013, and in a subsequent series of amplified treatments since, the latter a case presenting the folly of belief in the type of the standpoint of what is essentially merely **sense-perception per se** in type.

This brings us to the subject of "the immortals," the human species at its relatively present best.

As I shall explain the following choice, in due course here: the characteristic feature of the human species, is shown to us in two most crucial pieces of the evidence of revolutionary changes which a capable sort of actually human mind, when free, imposes upon both the human body and its functions.

The body wears out; but, the mind, when it actually functions, continues to struggle to perform its adopted mission, even when the mind has lost the means to perpetuate what it would have still possessed, had it not been caught up, so to speak, by an exhaustion of its mental strength and/or will. Thus, often, what the human intention had perpetuated as a continuation of that intention, that even a generation, several generations, or more after the death of the author. The discovery of physical principles, is typical of the ability of the presently deceased to have extended its role as an actively creative force, even in those exceptional cases, when the relevant author of that effort had been deceased for several or more generations. Nicholas of Cusa is an example of this immortal quality of achievement attained beyond the death of the subject person. The dead may thus live on, in effect, if not as living, but as if as angels.

So, were Max Planck and Albert Einstein, like Bernhard Riemann before them, each in their time.

Thus, as I have emphasized immediately above, *the human individual's role in society's life may be extended, in effect, even generations beyond the time of the person's actual demise, in such a manner.* Indeed, it should be the commitment of any person qualified to seek that outcome: *to create effects needed to be be-*

queathed on behalf of all mankind, even long beyond the actual death of the person's indivisible biological personality. The Christian Apostle Paul, emphasized that principle, as in the text of his inspiring Chapter 13 of **I Corinthians**.

The immediately preceding part of this present text, is to be treated as a prescribed validation of the intention which I had so just presented above. Yet, our Solar system does not stand still, nor do the effects of the passing, successive generations permit an actually fixed order of things within our Solar system: including such things which we might demand on behalf of a pre-fixed order of the planet, or a Solar system which we inhabit! The question to be asked, properly restated and answered again, is: does the planet we inhabit, make us, or, should our personal existence extend the purposed mission of planet Earth, or, again, should mankind's continued existence, as being mankind, shape the re-creation of the implied mission of the part of the universe which we inhabit?

Does the creative mission define its own cause? Or, is it not the developments of the Galaxy and Solar system, respectively, which shape the proper mission of the application of mankind's voluntary powers, to craft both the development and the prescribed mission of that development, even to within the extent of interplanetary developments among the planetary regions? Does Earth, or even the Solar system, predetermine its own destiny; or, does a higher order of an assigned destiny, define the future's choice of the shaping of the development of Earth, and also of the Solar system which we inhabit?

The Proper Answer

Consider the crucial hypothetical question:

We humans have repeatedly experienced the challenge of increasing the mean value of the energy-flux density of life lived on our planet Earth. This challenge has been subjected to two typical kinds of responses. Should we not choose to select the opinion, either that the changes in technology are caused by existing pre-disposition, or, that there is what appears to be a natural predisposition located within the already applied means for what we may define as "progress"—that in the specific sense of increased "energy-flux density" typical of the development of the human being?

In different forms of statement on this subject, the effect which we must associate with "increase of energy-flux density." might suggest to some, that the source of the required negentropy must have been provided by the Sun. However, the processes which we are considering here, are systemically anti-entropic. Also, to be considered, is the fact that the Solar system is regulated in large degree, by the regulatory role of the Solar system within its course in the galaxy.

More significant, is the fact that it is the human factor which mediates the role and limitations upon the manifest limits on entropy on planet Earth. More emphatically, the "steering" of the mediating factor considered, is an effect, chiefly regulated by the effects of decisions crafted by, and according to the development of the human minds, as the present prospect of a thermonuclear-fusion driver which is currently needed in the location of the Pacific region, that in which we are concerned presently, has predetermined the locations of the development of a thermo-nuclear-fusion driver-system which is to be built up.

Who, therefore, determines what, how, and why?

However, that does not complete my argument here.

The added sources of "energy" considered in that case, have been organized by human minds. Without the action of those human minds, there would be no negentropic, nor thermonuclear-fusion action to be reported, or experienced.

The consequence of that view applied to the subject-matter, is that the role of the human mind as such, is the principal, determining consideration. That leads us directly to consideration of the argument I had made for the Solar system's role more generally. The crux of the matter brings two considerations into focus. First, it is required that the Solar system, for example, be "a willfully intelligent system," in effect, rather than of a reductionist mode; mankind can supply that ingredient. It follows, that the principle of *mind per se* is a co-determining consideration which is being expressed in some mode.

The resulting consideration is, therefore, that the oligarchical system must be estimated, intrinsically, as something very close to Satanic, as was the Roman Empire, and like institutions which exhibit such negatives characteristically, and that most prominently, as London and Wall Street had made clear beyond any reasonable doubt.

II. Sense Deception

The unique distinction of the function of the human mind from all other known species, with their respective implications, is of such a nature, that we must neither encourage, nor deny the notion that there is a systemic distinction between the characteristically noëtic functions specific to the human being; even in respect to the qualities of the highest ranking creature of what has existed as merely animal life as such. The essential distinction of the actually human mind, from those of the beasts, is to be located by attention to the fact, that the mind of the human individual, and his, or her society, alike, share a faculty by means of which they are enabled to act *cognitively* to the combined effect, that *the human mind's innate potential ability is, to generate attempted actions based on the actual fore-knowing of a future, that which is expressed as a higher state of existence which is fairly, called "foreknowledge."*[5]

It is fair to say, if only off-handedly, that this uniquely human quality of actual existence serves as a means through which that human mind had been enabled to employ, and, to generate, and to impose upon itself, a qualitatively higher, ontological state of existing functions than had already existed in the "animal kingdom" otherwise.

However, this aspect of the matter, which is rightly named as foreknowledge, continues to suffer serious impediments, impediments which do not come to the human individual, as it were said, "with spontaneity," but, which arise chiefly, out from what seems to be a new-born quality of spirit which is to be recognized as unique to the human being. This **systemic distinction** of the human being is associated with some long-standing effects which must contend against the bestialization inherent in the oligarchical system's effective relative bestialization of not only the oligarchy itself, but which tends to be a numbing influence on the human species generally, a condition which requires the liberation of what had been the intended human victims of their own tendencies for submission to the influence of bestial follies otherwise specific to the oligarchical tendency.

That much now said, now turn our attention to the

crux of what should be fairly considered, at this late date, as "my life's work."

Now, Sense and Substance!

The most of those systemic errors of what has been known as associated with devotion to sense-perception *per se*, is the presumption, that because sense perception is what it pretends to be, as "sense perception:" a relatively great many human beings have fallen, as if prone to the popularized presumption, that sense-perception is simply equal to reality. Certainly, sense-perception does identify what seems to be all possible evidence which might be otherwise considered as "sense-certainty." Therefore, for a moment, it might be presumed, that, for this reason, the only apparent evidence contrary to human bestialization, falls under the heading of the concept of "the troubled human soul."

For as long as ordinary citizens might rely on the mental disorder to be known as sense-certainty, a certain refinement of the development of the individual's mind is needed to reveal, and perhaps cure the terrible mistakes which continue to be made as long as sense-perception is believed to be an underlying primary evidence respecting actually human behavior. The presumptions respecting sense-perception on that account, thus appear as essentially wrong opinions whose correction depends upon a sufficiently refined sense of those subject-matters of physical science which few citizens had taken the time and patience to consider critically.

There is some interesting evidence which should have warned almost anyone to consider some very serious questions leading toward increasing doubt in the belief that sense-perception "almost means" what is foolish mistakenly advertised as "sense certainty." The evidence of that foolishness of many human individuals, on that fact, is very, very strong, that on the best possible, but often overlooked, experimental grounds of evidence.

III. The Folly of Sense-Perception

This present chapter is supplied to serve for purposes of breaking the ground on which to settle some needed ground-breaking, which must be broken.

We must now shift our focus here, to emphasize additional, specifically human categories, beyond those which I have already referenced here above.

---

5. I.e., "foreknowledge" is a relatively commonplace capability of the most advanced quality of development of human individuals, as I have successfully "prophesied" on what has added up to have been a significant number of noted occasions.

Classical works of art are those rooted in "'the noëtic functions' of the human mind." Shown: Thomas Eakins, "The Cello Player" (1896).

These include specifically human sense-perception; which include (1) sense-perception as such, and the other, (2) the double meaning used to reference an existent principle of a state of life. The source of the often mistaken explanations associated with those two, just stated categories, presents doubts arising from any attempt to classify what those categories are commonly presumed to signify, as a matter of the notion of the precise identity and an existent efficiency of the physically-efficient definition of "life." That means the actual life of a human species, or that of the active life of the still-living, human individual. A very strong hint respecting the meaning of such subject-matters and their distinctions can be established. However, some groundwork is required respecting what all of this might actually be intended to mean *in the practice* of society. There is quite a lot to be sorted out on this account.

Against that back-drop, the most important, and also most defining functions of the human mind (and the living human body, too), are those which bear upon the specifically noëtic capacities of those mental functions of the human individual which pertain to the class of the activities pertaining, emphatically, to so-called "Classical artistic" functions. By that, I mean works of art rooted in the distinguishable principles of Classical artistic composition categorically, or, in other words, "the noëtic functions" of the human mind. On that ground of activities, the creative powers of the human mind, including the most significant of the intrinsically "non-linear" practices of truly "Classical" artistic composition, provide the essential basis for competent judgment respecting the actually "physical" expressions of physical-scientific practice.

The subject of the rather large portion of "fall-off in scientific insight" since the assassination of President John F. Kennedy, is typical of the effective symptoms of a "non-Classical," relatively bestialized practice. That means, specifically, the inherent failures induced by a more or less thorough reliance on the folly of "mathematical" systems. That is typical of the misuse of mathematics as such, as distinguished from a mathematics properly subordinated by a mission-commitment to underlying, "intrinsically non-mathematical" insights.

The emphasis is to be placed, in respect to matters of physical or comparable design of practice, on "non-linear" methods of practice. Accountants *per se*, are among the very worst choices in any seriously primary practice of applied financial-accounting methods—as the effectively evil habits of Wall Street firms, and related institutions, demonstrate that fact: "Mathematical physics" must, therefore, be, replaced in precedence, by an active notion of the "physical mathematics" which is premised on the methods of such, for purposes of illustration, as a Bernhard Riemann, a Max Planck, and an Albert Einstein, all that in rejection what has been actually the "hack work" of the likeness of a Bertrand Russell and his dupes among the merely mathematical physicists.

In other terms: insight into the principles of mind must be acknowledged as, by far, the indispensably superior authority properly reigning over mere mathematics *per se*. Accountants are sometimes useful—in their right place; but, as for accountants, their standard of practice has nothing to do with the functions associated with the principle of life, nor of actual principles of human practice, as such. Here, Classical artistic composition reigns supreme not only over mere mathematics, but in all matters with respect to human life as such. *The only true science, is that of the expert practice of human insight.*

Insight, itself, is exemplified by the effects of the

*practice of effectively increased degrees of "non-lin-
ear" energy-flux density: a physics rooted in its original foundations located in the work of such as Cardinal
Nicholas of Cusa, Johannes Kepler, and those in that
same tradition, as in the notable case of Alexander
Hamilton's characterization of the principles of the
American Economy. (I have "teased you, now," on
good grounds respecting what is now to follow.)*

The Folly of Arithmetic

As the infamous fraud of Euclid's argument shows,
the attempt to reduce reality to simply arithmetic systems, as in the notorious case of the common-place reductionists, such as Euclid and his co-thinkers, must
give way to the essential role of sets of actions which
are intrinsically, ontologically creative (i.e., *noëtic,
"spiritually"*) in their specifically physical-space-time
functions, rather than simply infinite-series-like, hence
"quasi-linear" projections.

The leading evidence which guides us to such con-
clusions as that, is typified in expression by the systemically anti-reductionist notion of a physical principle of life *per se*. The conclusive evidence to that effect,
becomes clear, when we have considered the relevant
distinction of the human life-form from that of lower
forms of what is also called "life."

For example, life is intrinsically a form of action, in
and of itself. The special significance of human life, as
to be distinguished from lower forms of life, is expressed efficiently by the actually "creative" forms of
willful intention specific to the human individual, as
shown by the effect of an idea which persists as efficiently as it continued to be an active factor of the author's intention, several generations, or more, after the
biological demise of the creative impulse located in the
rather long-deceased human discoverer.

A similar effect is expressed in products of truly
Classical artistic composition, and discoveries of valid
physical principle, alike.

Hence, the manifest "spill-over" to be recognized in
those persons who had effectively forecast actually
future events, as I have demonstrated that capability on
a significant number of historically notable occasions
which have been sprinkled among no less than fifty-odd
years of my life to present date. These include a number
of datings associated with publicized events which
have appeared publicly during the time preceding the
specific forecast in question.

Since such forecasts have transpired as they did, and
were publicized appropriately on that account, the ex-

periences to which I have referred aggregately here
now, indicate that "real lapsed space-time" is not simply
linear, but a much more "interesting" phenomenon. It
must be said, to similar effect, that the confidence of
some scientists in forecasting the realization of a forecast accomplishment, demonstrates that the past and
future of the experience of the individual's human life,
can not be competently reduced to a quasi-linear notion
of the "relativity" of the composition of physical space-
time in our universe.

The creative human personality has been able not
only to forecast future developments as if delivered by
Biblical prophets, but is enabled, sometimes, at the
least, to deal comparably with the past, similarly; that
is, the ability to recreate the past: the past which implicitly existed, but had not been recorded.

As for my own forecasting prowess: the first of the
particular forecasts to which I would be confident to lay
claim, occurred on pre-scheduled arrival with the significant breakdown crisis centered in the great U.S.A.
automotive bankruptcy of the late 1950s. From that
point on, there were subsequent great "crashes" in the
U.S.A., such as that of mid-Summer 1971, and then
beyond, including the forecast collapse of the Soviet
breakdown-crisis, and that of the U.S.A. over the entire
sweep throughout the continued trans-Atlantic breakdown-crisis of the span of the George W. Bush, Jr., and
the Obama administrations to the present date.

However, the "design" of such systemic economic
failures as those to which I have referred here now, had
come upon the world as a forecastable development
caused by the policies of the relevant nations and their
governments. What is most significant, practically, on
this account, is the simpler fact, that some people have
been capable of specific forecasts of future crucially
important events in history. What is obviously most significant about those events, is that some few nations,
and their members, even usually at the highest rank,
like the foolish President George W. Bush, Jr., and the
far more foolish President Barack Obama, would lead
entire nations and more to destruction as the role of
George W. Bush, Jr. and Barack Obama have been enabled to demonstrate the foolishness of relevant nations
and the majority of their governments, time, and time,
and time again.

The Use of Forecasting

I shall conclude this particular report with a rhetori-
cal question as to my here and now:

Why have most nations and their leadership failed,

both recklessly and often repeatedly, to respond effectively to the great crises whose onset had been readily forecastable by ordinary means, as the United States and most of Europe, at the least, this time around, once again? I, for example, have presented accurate warnings of major economic and related crises since the middle of the 1960s. Among the most notable examples of this, for the United States, for example, was the great breakdown-crisis of Summer 1971.

In the immediate aftermath of that Summer 1971 breakdown, the generality of the financial-economic spokesmen of the U.S. national system of that time, had frankly admitted that the leading cause for the failure of the financial-business community had been their own systemic error, in denying, even to themselves, that that crisis, which had been visibly oncoming since my widely circulated forecast to that effect in 1968, had been "inevitably" lacking in all the corrective fore-measures which had been actually available in advance.

Were all these leading business circles (of both western and central Europe, the United States, and so on, being simply stupid? That was not the kernel of the problem. My following exposition, will now point you to the actual factors of respectively cause and effect.

The "dominant system of empire throughout the planet today, was originally consolidated as the Seventeenth-Century Dutch imperial system," known today as the British Empire. Shown: Rembrandt's "The Syndics of the Drapers' Guild" (1662) depicts Amsterdam's merchants of the Dutch East India Company.

IV. The Principle of This Case

The core of the foolishness of the governments of such leading nations as the current Anglo-Dutch Empire-system (which controls under its own dominion, much of the nations of the world) is that it is a modern expression of the same oligarchical principle of all the greatest of the known empires of the planet. The behavior of such imperial oligarchical systems has conformed to the same most essential features of their characteristics for as far back as we possess systemically accurate knowledge of such imperialist entities. The fact of the matter presently, is that the dominant system of empire throughout the planet today, was originally consolidated as the Seventeenth-century Dutch imperial system, which, in turn, became extended to be known as (essentially) the same Dutch empire now also named as the British Empire.

The imperial system known to Europe, Africa, and adjoining regions, had emerged, for us moderns, from shadowy origins, but among the earlier of the typically clear examples of the nature of imperialism, is the well-proven case of the genocide conducted against the population of Troy. Most significant, is the fact of the imperial principle, which has, to the best of our knowledge, never been important as its part of anything other than, in essentials, an empire. The definition rests not upon quantity, but on systemic social-structural characteristics. The U.S.A.'s Wall Street, for example, is an instrument of imperial dictatorship, rather than being anything actually like a government of the U.S. people. Its characteristic is an imperial institution planted upon the United States by the Anglo-Dutch empire.

Since Wall Street's role as a branch of the Anglo-Dutch empire, rather than an actual agency practicing the role of a sovereign nation-state, Wall Street, which currently operates an imperialist tyranny upon and above the U.S.A. as a nation-state, has the same sort of impulse which Queen Elizabeth II practices with utter shamelessness. The intention of the Queen's empire, of which Wall Street is merely a subject, is to do as Elizabeth II had openly demanded: the reduction of the human population of the planet, from a declining level of seven billions of persons to one billion for the entire planet to share out, in the relatively immediate future. Those British imperial policies are now in effect, in measures, under, presently, British lackey Barack Obama, going into an accelerating rate of openly-declared genocide against the great majority of the U.S.A.'s own citizenry—a copy of Adolf Hitler's T-4 program of genocide, as I warned U.S. citizens publicly during Obama's first year in office.

That much said on that subject, what is my remedy for this criminal state of our nation's affairs?

What should have already been the indicated remedy for this presently evil state of affairs? Let us waste no time on lesser matters.

The elimination of the Wall Street system's wicked practices is the foremost requirement for the defense of our U.S. republic. The purpose of our nation's chief enemy, Wall Street, is precisely to conduct a financial looting process whose primary intention is to eliminate the majority of the U.S.A.'s current population. Only citizens, including presently elected ones, who are de facto lackeys of the mass-murderers, will tolerate Wall Street's continued tyranny within the United States. Hitler was a piker compared to Wall Street. No other interpretation will ever be accepted in the annals of actual history.

The Interest of the Nations

There should be no general policy among nations at this time, except the unity of existing sovereign nation-states, freed from financial oligarchism like that of the Anglo-Dutch tyranny, and intended to advance the conditions of life of nations and their people, according to a relatively urgent, future standard goal of global development of systems of thermonuclear fusion. The goal must take into account the urgency of bringing the immediate region of the Solar system, within the range of the region marked off by Earth and Mars, including the fields of asteroids, under control to obtain the needed security and development of that specific region, and to foster a human awareness of the dignity of its role in participation in necessary accomplishments to those ends in that spirit of achievements.

The systemic elimination of the oligarchical tyranny, is, then, simply an obvious imperative.